THE MUSIC, SONGS, &
INSTRUMENTS OF
IRELAND

KAREN FARRINGTON

THUNDER BAY
P·R·E·S·S

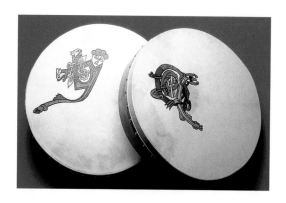

This edition published in 1998 by
Thunder Bay Press
5880 Oberlin Drive, Suite 400
San Diego, California 92121
1-800-284-3580

http://www.advmkt.com

Produced by
PRC Publishing Ltd,
Kiln House, 210 New Kings Road, London SW6 4NZ

ISBN 1 57145 154 4
(or Library of Congress CIP data if available)

1 2 3 4 5 98 99 00 01 02

Printed and bound in China

Previous page: *Traditional music at Bru Boru, Cashel, Co. Tipperary.*

Above: *Two bodhrán drums.*

Right: *A violin.*

$\mathcal{C}$ontents

$\mathfrak{I}$ntroduction

Irish traditional music is a neat and trim term for one large, unwieldy arena of style and sounds. It is a phrase used worldwide, yet the "Irish music" heard in the outback of Australia or the wilds of North America may well be unknown to the traditional musician in Ireland.

In turn, the music played by all three would be extraordinary to the ear of the Galway or Donegal harpers, pipers, singers, and dancers of centuries past. And remember that musical idioms, then and now, vary even between counties and districts of counties in Ireland! The history of Irish music—sometimes glorious, often troubled—sheds some light on how present-day traditional music has emerged. Much of what has gone before remains a mystery, and always will.

Irish traditional music stands mostly under the umbrella of folk music. The definition of folk music, according to the guidelines laid down by the International Folk Music Council in 1954, is: ". . . the product of a musical tradition that has evolved through the process of oral transmission. The factors shaping the tradition are a) continuity which links the present with the past; b) variation which springs from the individual or the group; c) selection by the community, which

Above: *Irish traditional music, in common with all folk music, has strong rural roots.*

Right: *Live performances, like this one by Blackthorn, are the impetus for the genre.*

were compelled to abandon their art—or face starvation. No longer could the traditional tunes be handed down as no one had the time or inclination to teach or learn them. Numerous well-loved numbers certainly became extinct and along with them perhaps the very essence of the music. Then, as now, musicians learned music by ear rather than sight so the notion of sheet music was an alien one. Without the evidence of notation it is impossible to tell just how traditional musicians once sounded.

Dr. Thérèse Smith, ethno-musicologist from University College, Dublin, elaborates on the oral tradition and its drawbacks. "We don't know anything about Irish traditional music until the collectors began to write it down. So we really can't trace the history back much further than nineteenth century. Until then concrete knowledge of the tradition is virtually unavailable.

"Even then, the collectors were trained in classical music and interpreted the music in classical terms.

"*Moore's Melodies*, written by the poet Thomas Moore in the early nineteenth century, are associated by the public with Ireland but this is not traditional music. They and many other ballads were composed by a largely Anglicized gentry, not the indigenous Irish population. In fact traditional singing tends to be unaccompanied.

"Regarding dance, the most popular forms seem to have originally been imports. The jig and the hornpipe were originally from England, the reel from Scotland."

The earliest evidence of Ireland's musical history now open to examination is scrappy, to say the least. In 1959 slate fragments bearing musical notation were discovered in the ruins of a church

determines the form or forms in which the music survives."

According to Zoltan Kodály, the champion of Hungarian ethnic music, folk songs are "the free, direct speech of the soul." Like food and drink, each culture produces its own, individual musical vogue but may have elements in common with one another.

All folk music tends towards a rural rather than an urban home. (Notwithstanding, some Irish ballads composed within the past 100 years are attached very soundly to towns and cities, reflecting a change in the social surroundings of working people, the life force of Irish traditional music.) The instruments used are easily portable and either cheap to buy or quickly made. In years past the music was never written down as it flourished before the days of print—or even pens. Rather, it was passed from generation to generation by word of mouth or from instrument to ear. A flourish might have been added here, a chorus there, as an air, jig, reel, or song proceeded down the line. The boundaries were constantly shifting.

And here we have the first obvious stumbling block in our definition of Irish traditional music. Three centuries ago Irish musicians suffered intolerable pressure, as we shall see, and many

Above left: *Queen Elizabeth I (1533–1603) issued one of her most famous decrees against Irish musicians. "Hang the harpers wherever found and burn their instruments." In no small way she helped to extinguish the art of harping on the small island.*

Right: *The problems caused by Elizabethan adventurers, the rampant protestantism of Cromwell and the Commonwealth, and the inequitable dealings with Irish Catholic lands seemed to have been solved with the accession of James II—a Catholic—to the English throne. Alas, it would lead to worse problems following James's defeat on the Boyne in 1689 (marked by the cross at right). What had taken place in the previous century, and what was to take place in the next, drove out many Irish and caused great discontinuity in the Irish oral tradition of music.*

near Smarmore, Co. Louth. They were scientifically dated to the second quarter of the fifteenth century. Only single lines of melody were shown but the notation was "measured," indicating that harmony existed at the time. This still leaves centuries of music cloaked in the mists of obscurity. For subsequent musical revivals were surely adulterated with the fashions of the day.

Before becoming dewy-eyed over the fate of Irish music, let's be clear. Change is inevitable and Irish traditional music was subject to it along with the music of the Dutch, Germans, Aborigines and Africans. For when the gateways of the world were opened by international travel musical styles were exported freely around the globe.

Ireland had for years been the subject of infiltrations and invasions, from the Celts through to the Normans and the Vikings, and it was a melting pot of customs. Later, the arrival of the English superimposed another culture which ultimately encroached on the existing one. Just as the Celts themselves were mixed and matched with other races, so was their music.

Many non-Irish people who found themselves in the delightful Emerald Isle during occupation failed to return home. Their brand of traditional music became absorbed into the native sounds and a new music evolved.

The Irish themselves traveled overseas, taking with them airs and ballads and bringing home foreign concepts which were incorporated into their own music. Consequently, a tune might be claimed as a traditional one by Ireland, Scotland and England—and no one knows where in truth it first originated. This cultural cross-fertilization left its mark.

Already we can see the musical genre which we are seeking to define is fluid in nature, perpetually gaining new songs and shedding the old.

Michael Rooney, from Irish festival organizers Comhaltas Ceoltóirí Éireann, is categoric. "In order to preserve the music there has to be a certain amount of change."

He points out that Seán Ó'Riada (1931–1971), one of the key revivalists of traditional music, nevertheless meted out some radical treatment to existing tunes.

"He composed and arranged music, added harmonies, put his personal print on it. In doing so he was up against the purists who didn't agree with his approach."

The tweaking of old tunes by new hands continues to be an irritant to a section of traditional musicians. However, it is the shape of things to come, according to Smith.

"Irish traditional music has gained popularity. Some groups have a wide audience. They tend to be groups that are quite experimental and in some ways some traditional musicians would no longer recognize them. But it is those willing to experiment who are bringing new life to the music."

The fear remains that, with increased communication, the regional styles will be merged to create one national style and Irish traditional music would suffer accordingly.

Today traditional musicians do little to help clarify the chaos of what is or isn't traditional. The music is informal, often impromptu, almost always improvised. Consequently, a tune may never sound the same twice. Traditional songs are given new words and may be known by two or many more titles. Within the confines of one tune a musical phrase may be played and then repeated with subtly different intonations. The scene is diverse. To capture traditional music and contain it is an exercise in wrestling with the wind.

Books and theses come a poor second to listening to the distinctive sound of the music. Indeed, the character of Irish music is impossible to convey with words, pictures, or musical notation. Smith sums up the appeal of Irish traditional music: "It has to do with social interaction. You cannot study traditional music in the same way as a Haydn symphony. The interest lies in the different variations and improvizations, in which musicians can develop their own sense of style."

Irish music is also Celtic music, although that title encompasses much more. Celtic music is the folk music of Ireland, Scotland, Wales, Brittany,

Right: *Famine, evictions, and flight from oppression: all these contributed to the Irish diaspora of the second half of the nineteenth century, taking Irish music to the world. Here, tenants on the Vandeleux estate in Kilrush, Co. Clare, are evicted during the late 1880s. The Royal Irish Constabulary stands by to protect the landlords' agents while they batter down the tenants' cottage wall to prevent reoccupation.*

The Celts

The cultural legacy of the Celts is still felt in the music of Ireland. They were a proud and resourceful people, inspired by conflict and the mysticism of the Druids. They established a way of life and language that persists even today.

Their arrival was gradual—over hundreds if not thousands of years—and their customs and skills became ingrained rather than imposed. For all the fearsome raiding of the Norsemen, and the brutally efficient Norman armies, it was the Celts who really shaped Irish society.

The Celts first defended Irish soil from invaders during the Viking wars, and they who mounted the first Irish attacks on foreign soil (their raids on western Britain during the third and fourth centuries A.D.). Where did they hail from?

At around 500 B.C. there was an aggressive race who occupied much of the Alpine region along with parts of central France and Spain. They were named the *Keltoi* by the Greeks and the *Celtae* by the Romans. Celtic speakers probably occupied pockets of land throughout Europe (including Ireland) early in the Bronze Age and continued migration would have established them further and further north and west.

The Celts shared a religious heritage and a broadly common language but there were also major differences between the tribes. The political order would range from large regional governments to kings commanding little more than a few settlements.

The Celts rattled the dominant Roman empire and the threat they posed spelled their fate. Only colonies on its fringes—Scotland, Wales, Western England, Brittany, the Isle of Man, and parts of Ireland—were left in relative peace to develop in their own distinctive ways. These sanctuaries remain the only places where the Celtic language is still spoken. That it has survived at all is largely thanks to pressures from nationalist groups in the areas concerned.

Much of the Celtic history remains a puzzle. The Celts left no records of their own. The picture we have is largely the product of archaeological imagery.

Celtic society in Ireland was a haphazard collection of family tribes, each ruled by a king.

These tribes would occasionally come together (perhaps for a council of war) to strike deals and form political alliances. There was no sense of any national identity.

Within the tribe, the pecking order was clearer. Beneath the king would come the warrior nobility, followed by those considered to have special skills—Druid priests, storytellers, artists, musicians, craftsman, and seers. Among the early Celts the king would have had strictly limited powers and any important decisions would have been taken by vote of all free men in the tribe. This semi-democracy seems to have broken down in later years with tribal leaders becoming more autocratic.

One significant aspect of Celtic feasting was the presence of a "praise poet," a bard who would recite songs and poems extolling the great deeds of the leading warriors and king. His purpose was to construct entertaining verse in three different veins—humorous, solemn, or sleep-inducing. In addition there would often be a satirist (a kind of court jester) as well. He would direct jibes at the personalities around him and was a much feared face at the table. It was to this privileged group that the early music-makers belonged.

When two armies met, the fighting could be delayed by several hours in a stand off in which a bizarre display of rituals was performed. Sometimes champions from each side would face each other in single combat, boasting loudly of their past victories, their bravery, their skills and their great ancestry.

Above it all a war chant would strike up, backed by the sound of sword on shield and swelled by the haunting sound of the battle horn or lurer. In this way the Celts hoped to unnerve their opponents and they were no doubt very often successful. Only in continental Europe, where the Celts found themselves up against highly disciplined, well-trained Roman legionnaires, did the tactic fail.

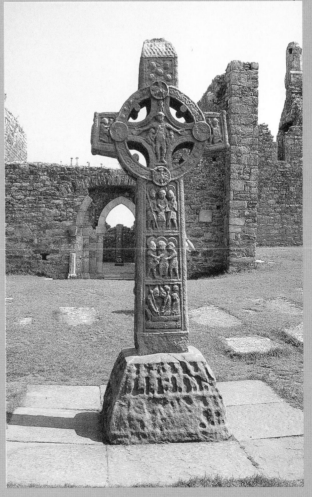

Galicia in Spain, Cornwall, the Isle of Man and parts of Canada. Celtic music traces its noble history from ancient to modern times. Its influence can be seen in church music, rock, jazz, and blues. The surge of support for traditional Irish music is sparking something of a backlash among other strands of Celtic music and has prompted accusations of "cultural imperialism" against the Irish, particularly among the Bretons and the Galicians.

Not all musicians from Ireland play Celtic music. And much Irish traditional music is played outside Ireland—although purists may claim that this, by definition, means it cannot be Irish and it becomes a matter of debate. Fundamentalists feel strongly that only songs sung in Gaelic can fall into the sphere of traditional music.

The Irish Traditional Music Archive (Taisce Cheol Dúchais Éireann), a non-profit making reference and resource centre in Dublin, aims to collect, preserve, organize, and disseminate information about Irish traditional music. It has encountered similar difficulties of definition and has adopted the admirable policy of trying to include rather than exclude material. So music may be deemed Irish and traditional by virtue of the location it is played in, the instruments it is played on, the nationality and inclination of the

Alfred Perceval Graves

Graves, one of the collectors of Irish traditional music, observed: "Ireland was the school of music for the Celts of Great Britain during the Middle Ages and her minstrels remained unrivaled until the Irish Bard, famous for 'the three feats' of solemn, gay, and sleep-compelling music, degenerated under the stress of the internecine conflict between Saxon and Gael in Ireland, and became the strolling minstrel, and finally the street ballad-singer."

players, the history of the piece, not to mention the overall style.

Given the streams which run into the rivers which run into the sea of Irish music we will take the modern view and insist that it is the feel of the music—its rhythm and momentum—that distinguishes it from others, rather than the district in which it is played or language in which it is sung.

Bearing all this in mind, the broad and loose term of Irish traditional music is something of a hallmark of the Irish Celtic character.

British composer Sir Hubert Parry (1848–1918), author of the famous choral song *Jerusalem*, opined: "Irish folk music is probably the most human, most varied, most poetical in the world and is particularly rich in tunes which imply considerable sympathetic sensitiveness."

Dr. George Petrie (1789–1866) was one of the few who aimed to preserve Irish traditional music for future generations by recording it. Sir William Stokes, his biographer, wrote: "It was Petrie's opinion that the music of Ireland stands pre-eminent among that of the other Celtic nations in beauty and power of expression, especially in her lamentations, and her love-songs; the latter, by their strange fitfulness and

Right: *Traditional music in Kilkenny: Uilleann pipes accompany Bodhrán, fiddle and accordion.*

Left: *Seán O'Casey was—according to himself—educated in the streets of Dublin. Born in 1884 at No. 85 Upper Dorset Street, he would teach himself Irish, join the Gaelic League and IRB, and write about Dublin during the troubles. Critical attacks on his last play drove him to England from 1926.*

Left: *Joaquin Rodrigo and James Galway.*

Right: *"The core performance is the pub session—which is a relatively new phenomena. Folk history puts the first pub session as being in London in the Holloway Road, within the past 50 years."* Today such sessions are ubiquitous.

sudden transitions from gladness to pathos and longing, are marked with a character peculiarly her own."

Playwright Seán O'Casey (1880–1964) felt that his native Ireland was "a kaleidoscope of astonishing contradictions," and that its music was a fine representation of paradox. He put it like this: "A people with one of the loveliest collections of folk music the world over . . . sing in season and out of season in tune and out of tune a national anthem so miserable in its conception of ordered sounds that a sparrow would be ashamed to warble it if he thought another sparrow were listening."

Ireland has for its national emblem the harp, a token of its proud musical heritage. It was centuries ago that St. Adamnan distinguished Ireland as the place: "Where the clerics sing like birds."

In more recent times Irish traditional music became the anthem of the rural folk drawn into the towns and cities. Later still, it was the unifying focus of the Irish abroad. It knew some bad times. In the middle of the century the Irish traditional music scene was gasping for air, virtually dead on its feet.

However, a revival of traditional music, which began in the 1960s, quickly mushroomed. Seán Ó'Riada was a prime mover. Coming from a different angle but achieving great results was Comhaltas Ceoltóirí Éireann. Comhaltas was formed in 1951 to promote Irish traditional music, song, and dance. It hosts more than forty Fleadhanna Ceoil, or festivals, each year and established a lively competition culture across Ireland.

According to Rooney: "This has really promoted the standard of Irish music and increased the number of people learning it. It was being played by very few people. Now lots of people are playing and it is in a very healthy state."

This small island is now as famous for its exciting musical scene as for its stout and shamrock. The nature of Irish traditional music, as we've already seen, means it can happen anytime, any place.

The music makers in Ireland have become so proliferate that in his autobiography, published in 1978, flautist James Galway quipped that it was impossible to toss a brick in the air in Galway without it landing on the head of a musician.

Now a new lament is being heard in Ireland regarding Irish music: not that there is too little of it but too much. To hear Irish music you might find yourself at an Irish pub, chains of which have sprung up across the world and even in Ireland itself. The Irish flavor—its "Guinness" mirrors, high bar stools and themed posters—are a part of a strategy to lure customers in.

To many "locals" in Ireland this seems a phoney and invasive culture. There are many

The first book on musical theory was written by Dublin-born William Bathe (1564–1614) and was published in 1584 while he studied at Oxford University. A revised edition, which appeared in 1600, informed the reader that it was: "A brief introduction to the skill of song, concerning the practice, set forth by William Bathe, gentleman. In which work is set downe ten sundry wayes of two parts in one upon the plain song. Also a table, newly added, of the comparisons of cleffs, how one followeth another for the naming of notes, with other necessarie examples to further the learner."

who roundly declare that music should only just be heard above the din of lively chatter. Another faction believes that music is only welcome in an Irish pub on St. Patrick's night and St. Stephen's night (Boxing Night). All other nights of the year should be devoted to conversation, an art in which the Irish take immense pride.

Niall Keegan, whose doctorate at the University of Limerick was entitled, "Communication Beyond Performance: Notation and Speech about Traditional Irish Music," puts traditional music into context. "It is a social music, traditionally in the background. Musicians can play but they don't really have to 'perform' for an audience."

Indeed, says Niall, musicians are somewhat taken aback when people do stop to listen.

"The core performance is the pub session—which is a relatively new phenomenon. Folk history puts the first pub session as being in London in the Holloway Road, within the past 50 years." It is this popular setting that gives Irish traditional music its immense strength.

"It has a huge amateur base. Few people playing traditional music are professional. They are doing so for the fun of it and they enjoy it just for its own sake."

In fact, professional musicians experience problems trying to draw audiences in Ireland. The biggest names in the traditional music business have no difficulties filling concert halls across the world while on their home ground they struggle to sell tickets.

This is because Irish people have numerous options to see bands in action. Invariably it's in the convivial surroundings of a local pub— obviously the preferred option, as it is free to enter and there's a choice of beverages on tap. So they feel no desire to part with money for tickets to sit in reverential silence amid the dry surroundings of an auditorium.

Below: *A fashion for dance halls, started in the 1920s in America, soon spread to Ireland where céilí bands provided the sounds. It was a radical departure from traditional music and dancing.*

It still surprises many to discover that the purpose of Irish music was, until recently, to accompany dance. Its exit from the dance hall and elevation to entertainment in its own right was pioneered by Ó'Riada.

"The music rarely, if ever, went without the dance," explains Keegan. "Ó'Riada put it in the concert hall. He had musicians in dress suits and put them on the stage.

"Ó'Riada's aim was to produce a true Irish art music, a highbrow music for Ireland. He arranged the tunes so they they were no longer suitable for dancing. Also, he revived eighteenth century harp music. Although the outcome was not just as he'd expected, Ó'Riada did turn traditional Irish tunes into listening music."

Ó'Riada was trying to resurrect a musical tradition that was in the doldrums. "It was being virtually ignored in Ireland," explains Keegan. "Irish music had become associated with poverty, illiteracy, and backwardness, as had the Irish language. It became closely related with the lifestyle of country people at a time when the nation was striving to modernize and compete internationally. This attitude is still sometimes found even today in Ireland."

Above: The shrine of St Mogue dating from the 11th century has helped historians to pin-point the arrival of the three-sided harp in Ireland.

Ó'Riada, a jazz pianist before his wholesale conversion to Irish traditional music, formed a group called Ceoltóirí Culainn which went on to become the Chieftains. In it he played the harpsichord, seeking to re-encapsulate a long lost sound.

Following in its wake came Planxty and The Bothy Band, two key groups of the 1970s. Planxty featured Christy Moore, who went on to become famous as a soloist, and Andy Irvine. The Bothy Band was directly influenced by Ó'Riada and, with its bouzouki riffs and harpsichord harmonics, set the standard of for traditional ensembles.

The successful revival in Irish traditional music can only be supremely beneficial to the young growing up in Ireland, if Czech composer Leos Janacek (1854–1928) is to be believed. He was himself greatly influenced by folk music and wrote: "Each folk song contains an entire man; his body, his soul, his surroundings, everything, everything. He who grows up among folk songs grows into a complete man."

Jnstruments

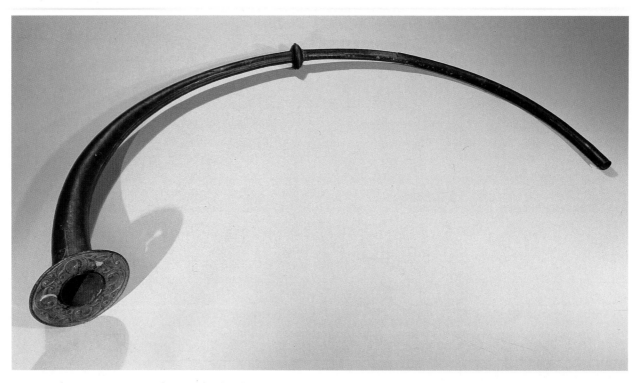

So what instruments bring forth that distinctive Irish sound? Foremost in the lineup comes the fiddle, a comparatively junior instrument in terms of musical ancestry but one that swiftly established itself. There's the Uilleann pipes which mark out any piece of music in which they are played as typically Irish. Add in the wind section—tin whistle and wooden flute—and percussion (only the Bodhrán will do) and the medley begins to take shape. The back row generally features the concertina, accordion, latterly the bouzouki, and sometimes the guitar. Early recordings of Irish traditional music made in the 1920s in America included the piano. It isn't a permanent feature today. On its own stands the harp, the epicenter of Irish music and yet so often relegated to second division status today.

One of the oldest instruments in Ireland is the bronze Loughnashade Horn, dredged from the floor of a lake in County Armagh. One of four horns discovered at the same time with typically Celtic decoration, it is thought to have been submerged as part of a religious offering in the Iron Age when Ireland was on the brink of conversion to Christianity. The horn is in the National Museum of Ireland.

Above: *Pulled from the floor of a lake in Co. Armagh, the Loughnashade Horn is one of the oldest instruments in Ireland.*

Right: *Pub musicians creating a distinctively Irish sound.*

Harp

The harp has evolved with a vividly colorful history, and nowhere more so than in Ireland. Here the harp was revered and harpers were little short of heroes until they became victims of political pressure. At the same time new and more complex musical works demanded greater flexibility among instruments, a versatility that harps of the era could not offer. By the 1800s harps were a whisper away from extinction. It was nearly 200 years before the Gaelic harp was once again musically valued, thanks to the revival in the traditions of Irish music.

Harp history begins back in the far reaches of time when man first discovered that a taut string, when plucked, would bring forth a pleasing sound. There were harp-style instruments discovered in the "Royal Cemetery" at Ur in Mesopotamia which date back to 2500 B.C.

A strong association was forged between the harp and Christianity because it appeared so frequently in biblical imagery. King David was reputedly an accomplished harp player and it became the instrument most closely linked to God's angels.

In the Bible, within Revelation, we learn: "And I heard a voice from heaven, as the voice of many waters, and as the voice of a great thunder: and I heard the voice of harpers, harping with their harps. And they sung as it were a new song . . . and no man could learn that song but the hundred and forty and four thousand which were redeemed from the earth."

John Milton's *Paradise Lost* further reinforces the celestial connection:

Then, crowned again, their golden harps they took
Harps ever tuned, that glittering by their side
Like quivers hung; and with preamble sweet
Of charming symphony they introduce
Their sacred song, and waken rapture high

No voice exempt, no voice but well could join
Melodious part; such concords as in heaven.

Just how the harp made its way to Ireland nobody knows. A triangular harp appears in Scottish stone reliefs in the ninth century. It was probably exported to Ireland, although four-sided harps, or lyres, appear to have been the norm there at that time. As far as we know the triangular harp had crossed the water by the tenth century and perhaps much earlier.

The word harp is derived from Anglo-Saxon, German, and Norse words, meaning "to pluck." In Gaelic, the term for a wire-strung instrument, including the harp, was a *cruit*. Later both Scots and Irish people knew a harp as a *clarsach* or *clairseach*.

Alas, Brian Boru's harp—otherwise known as the Great Harp—the oldest Irish harp in

Above: *Turlough O'Carolan, "The Irish Bard," was a popular traveling minstrel well loved for the planxties or verses that he put to music.*

Right: *The image of Ireland from the days of Henry VIII— a triangular harp.*

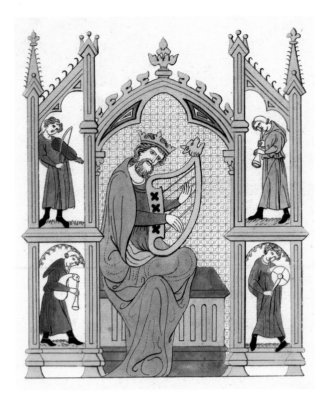

existence which now resides at Trinity College, Dublin, is something of a red herring. Brian Boru, the self-styled "Emperor of the Irish," was an antihero killed at the Battle of Clontarf on Good Friday in 1014 as he fought—and triumphed—against a coalition of Irish tribes and Vikings. However, the harp at Trinity postdates that battle by several centuries. It was almost certainly made during the fourteenth century.

As a matter of interest it is no more a "Great" harp than one that once belonged to Brian Boru. It stands but 70 centimetres or 28 inches high. For the record, it has 29 brass strings and a soundbox carved from a solid section of willow. Tradition dictated that the Irish harps were wire-strung rather than having strings of gut or twisted hair and were played with long fingernails instead of fingertips. (However, it's a modern myth to suggest that all harp players of yesteryear used curling talons to play. Minstrels who played other instruments in addition to the harp would have been unable to fulfill such a requirement.) The result was a distinctive bell-like sound.

A sister of the Great Harp exists in the National Museum of Antiquities in Edinburgh. The Queen Mary Harp, made in about 1500, is deemed to have been crafted by the same maker or at least copied from the original.

Some straightforward historical detective work does, however, place the harp in Ireland during Boru's era. It is depicted on an eleventh century plaque in the National Museum decorating the shrine of St. Mogue. In 1215 the imprint of a harp appeared on coinage produced in Dublin. The Welsh king Gruffydd ap Cynan (1054–1137), who was born and bred in Ireland, is said to have introduced the harp to Wales.

And the Italian poet Dante (1265–1321) bequeathed some telling observations about Irish harping:

"This most ancient instrument was brought to us from Ireland, where they are excellently made, and in great numbers, the inhabitants of that island having practiced on it for many ages. Nay, they even place it in the arms of the kingdom and paint it on their public buildings and stamp it on their coins, giving as a reason their being descended from the Royal Prophet David"

It is worth pointing out here that at the time the harp was in the coat of arms of Leinster alone. Only from the age of Henry VIII in the early sixteenth century did it feature as the national symbol of all Ireland.

Giraldus Cambrensis, a traveling cleric, leaves us this double-edged compliment for the twelfth century Irish:

"I find among these people commendable diligence only on musical instruments, on which they are incomparably more skilled than any nation I have seen. Their style is not, as on British instruments to which we are accustomed, deliberate and solemn, but quick and lively; nevertheless the sound is smooth and pleasant. It is remarkable that, with such rapid fingerwork, the musical rhythm is maintained and that, by unfailingly disciplined art, the integrity of the tune is fully preserved throughout the ornate rhythms and profusely intricate polyphony . . ."

Another tribute to the skill of Irish harpers was made in the late fourteenth century by Vincenzo Galilei, father of the astronomer Galileo. He was particularly impressed at the quality of those harps made in Ireland which, as

a musician, he had occasion to play. He was equally delighted by the pipers.

Polydore Virgil, who lived in England in the first half of the sixteenth century, noted: "The Irish practice music and are eminently skilled in it. Their performance, both vocal and instrumental, is exquisite but so bold and impassioned, that it is amazing how they can observe the rules of their art amidst such rapid evolutions of the fingers and vibrations of the voice; and yet they do observe them to perfection."

Harps, then, were an essential feature of Irish life as it entered the second millennium and harpers were duly respected for their skills.

And for some 600 years a set of nimble fingers and an ear for a tune would take a person far in Ireland. It was the aristocrat of instruments, providing music for the upper echelons of society. Harp music was not the music of the peasantry—which went on to be the body of traditional music. That historical factor continues to set harp music slightly apart from traditional. Harpers were welcomed at the highest tables in the land, around which they had the ear of the nobility. It frequently fell to them to comment on matters diplomatic or military. Along with

According to Irish mythology the God Dagda of the Tuatha overcomes his enemies thanks to the three musical feats of the harp. The *goltrai*, which inspires weeping; the *geantrai*, which causes laughter, and the sleep-inducing *suantrai*.

bards, the eulogizing poets of old Irish courts, they were accorded titles and wealth in recognition of their services. These were not passed down to their children in an hereditary fashion but were awarded to the best harpers who followed in their wake. However, their days of dominance were numbered.

Irish culture was turned inside out with the English plantations which began in Tudor times. There was much about life in Ireland which horrified the incoming English and Scots, not least the presumptions of the musicians exemplified by the harpers. They became something of a symbol of all that was apparently rotten in this little island which the invaders glibly believed to be uncultured and barbaric. Also the immigrants realized the sound of the harp, together with the pipes, could quickly become a rallying point for the oppressed Irish.

A campaign against the harpers began and was enthusiastically backed by the English Queen Elizabeth I. "Hang the harpers wherever found and destroy their instruments," she proclaimed in 1603. Ironically both she in England and Lord Barrymore in Ireland, to whom she made the savage declaration, both employed harpers in their households. Robert Devereux, second Earl of Essex, who fell from grace with Elizabeth after failing to suppress the 1600 uprising in Ireland, similarly kept a harper. It is said that the excellent harper Robert Cruise was part of the earl's household. Stanihurst, a respected commentator of Tudor times, sang his praises.

"In these days lived Cruise, the most remarkable harper within the memory of man. He carefully avoids that jarring sound which arises from

C.H.S. del.   *Aquatinted by R. Havell.*

A British Bard   and an Ovate.

Left: *Harpers knew a unique place in Irish society. So privileged was their position that they could talk freely with all ranks, from lord to pauper.*

Right: *A craftsman at the Clark Instrument Company in New York devotes his skill to the construction of an orchestral harp.*

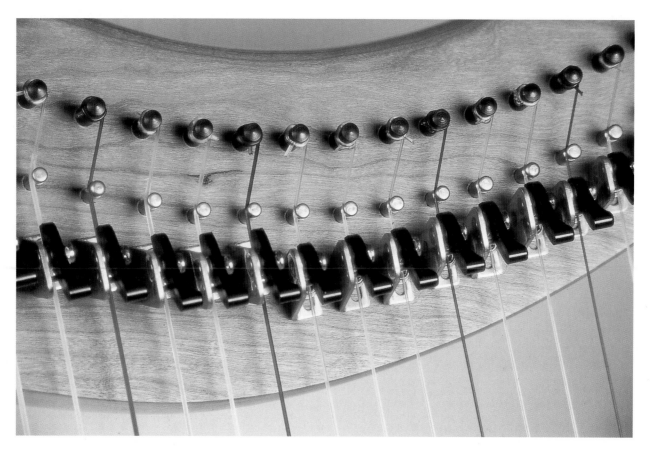

Above: *The fine detail of the modern harp's tuning mechanism reveals how technically advanced the instrument has become.*

unstretched and untuned strings and, moreover, by a certain method of tuning and modulating he preserves an exquisite concord which has a surprising effect upon the ears of his auditors, such that one would regard him rather as the only, than the greatest harper."

Cromwell continued the same theme of repression begun by Elizabeth, and during his short tenure in Ireland, 500 harps were confiscated and incinerated in Dublin alone.

That antagonism set in train a chain of events which virtually eradicated the tradition of harping in Ireland. Catholic landowners had their property confiscated and the estates became rich pickings for incoming English and Scottish nobility. Prosperous patrons were soon in short supply. Harpers, who had been top of the social pile, found themselves among the lower orders, struggling to survive. Graceful fingernails, which once plucked out a thrilling tune, were worn away with manual toil. The daily crusade to keep hunger at bay left little time for the luxuries of life, like harp-playing or tuition for the next generation. One by one the tinkling harps of Old Ireland were extinguished. The few that clung to

their art were compelled to become wandering minstrels, begging food and shelter wherever they could.

As poet Thomas Moore (1779–1852) noted in his 1807 work entitled *Irish Melodies*:

The harp that once thro' Tara's halls
The soul of music shed,
Now hangs as mute on Tara's walls
As if that soul were fled.

Aibhlìn McCrann, secretary of Cáirde Na Cruite, or Friends of the Harp, in Dublin likens the hounding of the Irish harpers three hundred years ago to the ethnic cleansing that has gained so much notoriety in the twentieth century.

"Harpers were persecuted because their high status, which allowed them into the most influential company in the land, had them well-placed for spying.

"Like the poet the harper also had the power of satire. Ruthlessly used, this could destroy the reputation of a victim and make his life all but impossible in the vicinity thereafter.

"The Gaelic civilization pre-1690 was a system of patronage. Chieftains and kings had poets and harpers in their retinue. This continued under the Anglo-Irish and harpers traveled between big houses. The patrons would have been of Anglo-Irish stock. Once the native Irish and the Anglo Irish were stripped of their land and houses, there was nowhere for the harpers to go."

Other factors, apart from those inspired by the migrant English and Scots, brought pressure to bear on the harp, too. It was difficult to modulate or re-tune harps to accommodate the variety and complexity of musical works now being created. Their inflexibility played a part in the decline of harping. The fretted lute or violin was favored in its place.

The harps that endured housed more strings and were therefore bigger, a discouragement to the itinerant harper who carried his instrument with the rest of his belongings on horseback.

That harp playing endured at all was probably because it was one job eminently suited to the blind. Repression or no repression, there were few opportunities otherwise available to them.

Blindness brought about by an attack of smallpox at the age of eighteen brought Toirdhealbhach O Cearbhallain to the harp. Throughout his illustrious career he was better known as Turlogh O'Carolan—or simply Carolan.

Born in a town called Nobber, Co. Meath, Carolan (1670–1738) was the son of a black-

smith. At the age of about fourteen Carolan's father John took his family to Ballyfarnon in the west of Ireland where he worked for the distinguished MacDermott Roe family. Even before he was struck down by smallpox the young Carolan had so impressed Mrs. Maire MacDermott Roe that she gave him some formal education.

Carolan was lucky to survive the ravages of the disease. Once again Mrs. MacDermott Roe interceded on his behalf, this time by apprenticing him to a harper to whom she was related. For three years Carolan studied the instrument before setting off, aged twenty-one, with harp, horse, and guide. Like other traveling musicians of the day, he was given hospitality at the castles and estates of Ireland where he—quite literally—sang for his supper.

He was hampered in his mastery of the harp because he started to play so late in life. However,

Below: *The remains of Carolan's harp at Clonalis House. His talents with music and words earned him the title of "Irish bard."*

he soon added the composition of musical verse to his repertoire, which increased his popularity. Carolan put words to the melodies he wrote—mostly in Irish but occasionally in English—and dedicated them to his hosts. He called these ditties "planxties," a term it is thought he made up, meaning, "verse to honor." Here are the first and last verses of a planxty written for one Fanny Power:

I wish to speak of a gracious young lady,
A loveable lady of beauty and reputation,
Who lives in the town near the bay of Loch Riabhach.
I'm thankful that I had the chance to meet her.

May I not leave this world, if I may be so bold,
Unless I can first cheerfully dance at your wedding
feast.
I challenge the one who would ever ask a dowry for
you,
O Pearl-Child of white hands.

Apart from being a skilled musician Carolan distinguished himself as something of a ladies' man and "bon viveur." Jonathan Swift (1667–1745), the author of *Gulliver's Travels* who met Carolan in Dublin was moved to comment: "He is a man who is able to drink!"

As a testament to his love of drinking, Carolan wrote the following ode:

O Whiskey, heart of my soul!
You always knock me down.
I'm without sense, I don't know where I am!
You'd think that I'd take the warning.
My coat is all torn up and I lost my cravat because of
you.
But let all you've done be forgiven,
So long as you meet me again tomorrow!

Yet Charles O'Conor, a pupil and friend of Carolan's, was quick to defend him against charges of over-indulgence. Carolan did drink, admits O'Conor, "a habit which he imagined added strength to the flights of his genius.

"In justice, it must be observed that he was seldom surprised by intoxication. Constitutionally pious, he never omitted daily prayers and fondly imagined himself inspired when he composed some pieces of Church music. Gay by nature, and cheerful from habit, he was a pleasing member of society whilst his talents and his morality procured for him esteem and friends wherever he visited."

It was as much for his good humor, wit, and generous spirit as his music that Carolan was so well-received around Ireland.

At 50 Carolan married Mary Maguire, described at the time as "a young lady." They lived at Mohill, Co. Leitrim and had six daughters and a son. The boy became a harper like his father, although never knew the same success. A book of tunes once believed to have been written by Carolan senior has since been attributed to the son who ran away from Ireland with a married woman and made a new life for himself in London where he worked as a harp teacher.

Left: *Irish harper Mary O'Hara pictured with her instrument in 1956.*

Right: *Irish traditional music at Bru Boru, Cashel, Co. Tipperary.*

Carolan outlived his wife by five years. In 1738 he returned to the MacDermott Roe Estate in Roscommon to die. He called for his harp and played his final piece, "Farewell to Music," before retiring to bed in exhaustion. Before he passed away he called for a drink of whiskey, his favorite tipple. Allegedly, his last words were thus: "The drink and I have been friends for so long, it would be a pity for me to leave without one last kiss."

He was buried in the churchyard at Kilronan. His funeral thronged with rich and poor, English and Irish. For Carolan, as "the last of the great Irish bards," had avoided falling into any political camp. He played for Catholic or Protestant, indeed, anyone who would part with money for his services.

At least 200 of Carolan's compositions survived him. More than half the pieces in the earliest surviving collection of Irish music, *A Collection of the Most Celebrated Irish Tunes proper for the Violin, German Flute, or Hautboy*, published by John and William Neale in Dublin in 1724 are by Carolan.

However, most are in the form of a single line and how he harmonized is purely a matter of conjecture. Critics dismiss Carolan's work for its European bias. It is likely that Carolan met the Italian violinist Francesco Geminiani (1679–1762) who lived in Dublin. At least they are sure to have encountered one another's work. Carolan built this influence into his songs, which were written against a traditional Irish background. The blend is epitomized in "Carolan's Concerto," a grandly-titled composition, still falling some way short of an orchestral concerto, and it is for this work that he is most often remembered today.

To mark the 250th anniversary of his death in 1988, the people of Nobber organized a Harp and Cultural festival which has since become an annual event, held in October. So successful was revival of the harp culture that "The Meath Harp School" was established in Nobber in 1993.

By the dawn of the nineteenth century the heyday of Irish harping was finished. There were

Right: *A recent boom in the popularity of Irish traditional music means that advertised performances can draw enormous crowds.*

nevertheless some concerted efforts to save the noble art from oblivion.

An Irishman living in Denmark, James Dungan, agreed to finance a harp festival at Granard in 1781. Seven harpers attended and one Charles Fanning won the first prize of ten guineas. Arthur O'Neill (1734–1816), blind from the age of eight, was in second place and received eight guineas. (O'Neill was famous for having played the newly-strung Great Harp through the streets of Limerick in 1760.) The festival at Granard was repeated four more times, the last, in 1785, attracting an audience of more than a thousand people.

Seven years later a harp celebration was organised by the Presbyterian's in Belfast which attracted ten Irish entrants and one Welsh one. Of the Irish ten, six were blind. Once again, Fanning was the victor and O'Neill was in second place.

However, this harp festival was significant not because of the winners but thanks to an also-ran, Denis Hempson, and a paid observer by the name of Edward Bunting who pioneered the trend of collecting old tunes for posterity.

Hempson (1695–1807) is one of the few people ever whose lifetime spanned three centuries. Born in Craigmore, Co. Derry, he was blind from the age of three, also after an attack of smallpox. At the time of the Belfast Harp Festival he was an amazing ninety-seven years old, still playing in the traditional manner with harp held to his left shoulder and spiney fingernails on his right hand plucking the lower strings while the left hand played the upper strings. At the time he declared: "When I played the old tunes, not another of the harpers would play after me."

From Hempson's point of view, traditional harping was already doomed as none of the musicians he observed were faithful to the style he knew from boyhood. Despite Bunting's best efforts to coax and cajole Hempson refused to pass on tricks of his trade for the record because he felt the techniques were too complex and demanding for the young harpers of the day who were already playing gut-strung instruments. He was so steeped in old-style music that he regarded Carolan as distinctly avant garde.

Hempson played a harp which had been made in 1702 by Comac O'Kelly. It was this harp which he took to Scotland where he introduced some traditional Irish airs for the first time to an eager audience. (Exchanges like this have made the tracking of traditional Irish melodies through history notoriously difficult.) On the side of Hempson's harp were inscribed the words:

In the time of Noah I was green
Since his flood I had not been seen
Until seventeen hundred and two I was found
By Cormac O'Kelly underground
He raised me up to that degree
The Queen of Music you may call me.

Schools for harpers were begun with the best intentions—of providing the blind with a valuable skill and the preservation of music. Each venture failed as the appalling social conditions threw up more pressing priorities.

Traditional harp playing limped on for only a short while after 1800 when the European pedal harp, the forbear of today's orchestral harp, was introduced to the island. Now it was this harp which found favor in the drawing rooms of the wealthy. Its maker in Ireland, John Egan of Dublin, produced an alternative which helped keep the memory of traditional harping alive. The "Royal Portable Irish Harp," dating from about 1819, exchanged pedals for single action ditals or finger keys. It was played with the fingertips and therefore sounded very different to its predecessor. Now it became an instrument for women rather than men, played among the middle classes.

Given the political woes of Ireland at the time, the image of the "last Irish harpist" became a powerful focus for the nationalist movement, amply expressing the squeeze being put on native culture.

McCrann testifies that there has recently been a huge renaissance in the harp, "It is a key part of traditional music."

She adds, "The gut-strung harp is akin to a classical harp in an orchestra. The wire strung harp is like a cross between a harpsichord and a

Right: *Harps are generally too large to feature in pub sessions but have nevertheless earned their place in the traditional music played in more formal settings.*

Spreading the sweet sounds of the strings in an unexpected quarter, harp-player Daphne Hellman became one of New York's best known buskers. The daily trawl home for commuters at Grand Central Station was frequently brightened by Hellman's beautiful music.

The daughter of a wealthy Irish banker, Hellman wanted for nothing as she grew up in American high society, eventually coming out as a debutante. Sixty years and three husbands later her abiding passion was still the harp, an instrument she first played at age twelve. She remained wealthy, with summer homes on Long Island and Cape Cod, but busked even as an octagenarian, simply for the love of the harp.

steel strung guitar, with resonance. It is so resonant that each string has to be stopped after it is played to curtail the sound—called damping.

"There are various styles of damping. Essentially harpers use the flat palms of both hands or the finger next to the one which has just played.

"There is no plectrum in harp-playing. Players use the thumb and the first three fingers to pluck the strings. The fifth finger (little finger) is not used.

"There is a huge resurgence in Ireland and there is as much interest coming from abroad as there is here, particularly in Brittany, Wales, and America."

Further barriers still remain which limit the number of students. Children aged about nine can start learning to play but the major drawbacks are the huge cost of the instrument and its lack of portability. It costs about ten times as much as a basic guitar which has become a more common option. Although the harp's popularity is growing there is still a shortage of teachers and the expertise is focussed in a few places rather than being widespread.

The revival has centered mostly on the modern descendants of the traditional Irish harps. Laurence Egar, of Gardiners Hill in Cork, is one of a handful of harp-makers in Eire. A graphic designer by training, he turned his hobby of harp-making into his life's work to supply a burgeoning demand.

He makes Neo-Irish harps, those with gut or nylon strings rather than brass. This means they can be played with fingertips rather than nails.

Each harp stands a little more than four feet high (1.1 meters) and takes about two months to make. It has thirty-four strings compared with the forty-six or seven to be found on orchestral harps, so the range of the Neo-Irish harp is limited but nevertheless pleasing. His harps are played in pubs and at weddings in celebration of Irish traditional music or even in classical recitals.

"For the frame I use hardwoods like elm, maple or oak. For the soundboard I use spruce, in common with all stringed instruments.

"Harp playing is getting more popular because there are good teachers available now."

One of those teachers is American-born Bonnie Shaljean who settled first in England and then in Ireland. Although her great-grandparents were Irish and emigrated to the States she heard classical and pop music at home rather than traditional Irish sounds. It was when she lived in a district of London dominated by Irish culture that she swapped her classical piano playing for that of the harp.

"I love the sound it makes. Making that sound is pure magic. I enjoy Irish traditional music, all kinds of folk music and Renaissance music too.

"The standards of playing and instrument making have gone up a lot. It is still not played as much as the guitar or the fiddle but people playing are playing better, on better instruments."

It is possible to competently pick out a tune on the harp after just a year of tuition. To comprehend the nuances can take up to twenty years.

Attempts to recreate the sound and scene of years ago are more or less doomed to failure. Too little information of substance has been passed down for interpretation. The harps being made today and the tunes being plucked upon them would barely be recognized by the traditional players of years ago.

Right: *To study the fine detail on the tuning mechanism of a double action harp is to glean the complexities facing today's players.*

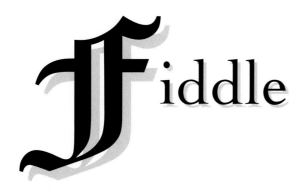iddle

One mischievous definition insists that the fiddle is "an instrument to tickle human ears by friction of a horse's tail on the entrails of a cat."

This evokes a shudder before the much-maligned instrument is even in hand. In fact dextrous use of the fiddle by a host of players in Ireland has helped to elevate it to something of the king pin in national music. The fiddle is the twin brother of the violin, though instead of being used for orchestral symphonies, it is applied to folk or traditional music. Techniques of playing between the two may vary, and not just between symphony violin and folk fiddle. There are even different methods that distinguish traditional music players; these are usually defined by the locality from which they come.

Fiddles tend to have steel strings. Generally speaking, bows for traditional music are some-times left slack while instruments may be tuned either below or above concert pitch.

A relative latecomer to the scene, the violin descended from the rebecs and viols of medieval times. English King Charles II signaled its ascendancy when he returned to his court after exile in France where violins knew great popularity. He installed a band of twenty-four violin players to serenade him at mealtimes. Lighter and brighter than the viol which preceded it, the violin was better suited to the Italian music which was the listener's choice at the time.

Below: *Grafton Street in Dublin comes alive with the sound of music when the buskers strike up. Visitors love it as the sound is quintessentially Irish.*

Right: *Dvorak violin, front. The violin is in the same family as the viola, cello and double bass. Their country cousin is the fiddle.*

Left: *Violin, back. A relative latecomer to the scene, the violin descended from the rebecs and viols of medieval times.*

Right: *The fiddle's four strings are tuned by tightening or loosening pegs.*

Below right: *The base of the strings is in close proximity to the chin rest.*

The seventeenth and early eighteenth century became the heyday of the violin makers, pre-eminent among them Nicola Amati (1596–1684) and his pupil Antonio Stradivari (1644–1737), better known as Stradivarius.

Just why fiddle-playing gained such a firm foothold in Ireland remains a mystery. Before the advent of the violin in Ireland there was the tympan, a stringed instrument played with a bow.

Rab Cherry, a fiddle player and maker from Belfast, explains what little is known of the tympan. "In its earliest days it would have been a plucked instrument. Some time around the tenth century the bow was invented and there has probably been a bowed instrument in Ireland since the eleventh century."

Little is known about what music was played on the tympan and just how it sounded. History has no record of its virtues or its drawbacks.

"Whatever had previously been used was superseded and the violin took its place," says Cherry.

Perhaps another important link that drew the violin into Ireland was the liking that Italian composer Francesco Geminiani (1687–1762) developed for Dublin, where he lived for many years and ultimately died. Geminiani is thought to have brought with him to Ireland the latest style of playing the violin, which he himself learned at the knee of virtuoso Arcangelo Corelli (1653–1713).

Violins were embraced by both rich and poor. There is little evidence of resistance among the rural nationalists to use of the instrument which became de rigeur in the drawing rooms of Dublin high society in the first half of the eighteenth century. However, in the city it reflected English and European styles of music in its playing while in the countryside it was adapted for traditional tunes.

Three of the most admired fiddlers of the century were Michael Coleman, James Morrison, and Paddy Killoran, all of whom emi-

grated to America before producing their finest recordings. Coleman particularly won global recognition for his skills. Ó'Riada called him "a brilliant virtuoso" but lamented the temptation among many fiddlers who followed afterwards to imitate him rather than seek their own style.

Each region has honed its own fiddle style. The lyrical Sligo style, which is slower in pace than the music of Donegal but faster than that of Clare, is strongly identified in the recordings of Michael Coleman.

Clare's style of fiddling, which emphasizes finger ornamentation rather than bow work, was made familiar through the Comhaltas organization as it was often played in festivals and competitions.

In Ireland, Padraig O'Keefe (c. 1888-1963) passed on the techniques known in the Sliabh Luachra country, on the Cork-Kerry border, to scores of pupils.

Perhaps the most distinctive of the regional styles is that of Donegal where an aggressive staccato attack on the strings has been fostered by its fiddlers. While their counterparts in the south are more gently flowing, the Donegal fiddlers—and those who imitate the style—set off at a hard-driving rapid pace. The emphasis is on bowed rather than finger ornamentation. Thanks to its close proximity, Donegal fiddlers have been widely influenced by those in Scotland which also knows the no frills, "up-and-at-'em" way of playing. Indeed, Scottish tunes, or Irish versions of them, feature prominently in the repertoire of many Donegal fiddlers alongside Strathbeys, polkas, Highlands, and Germans. There is nevertheless the ability to sound sweet, like fiddlers Frank Cassidy and Danny O'Donnell.

Within the framework of Donegal fiddling is room for various individual styles and there is no single correct Donegal style; according to Cherry. "You could get three players from Donegal who all sounded different. The style of southwest Donegal is distinct from the northwest and the east is different again. Donegal fiddle music was very much the poor relation of Irish fiddle playing until recently." Now, it has a thriving base when other fiddle styles are beginning to lapse into obscurity.

Cherry places importance on style rather than technique in fiddle playing.

John Smithwick Wayland, a piper in the early 1900s, became frustrated with the surge of popularity for the fiddle. In response he wrote a song to vent his feelings, called "The Warpipes versus the Fiddle."

Said the fiddle to the warpipes, "You're made up of drones
You can boast of but one octave and you have no semitones."
Said the warpipes to the fiddle, as his eyes now flashed with fire,
"For untruthfulness and impudence you come second to the LYRE
You mentioned just a while ago about my arms and legs
But you can boast of none at all for you have only pegs
And what is more, I say sir, that your head is only glued
And anyone can see sir, that you're very often screwed."
Said the fiddle, "I've a belly and a back and sides, moreover,
And a shift or two at intervals, my nakedness to cover;
I've a head-piece and a tail-piece, and though I'm often tight,
I've a bridge to rest my bones upon when I retire at night;
My audience I can move to tears, with feelings of emotion
Without using golden syrup or any other lotion . . ."

"Modern players have a problem with styles. Styles are something that develop over a long, long period of time. They are generally developed by people who play as a pastime. They don't practice five hours a day. They have neither the time nor the inclination to develop a wide range of techniques. A lot of people spend a lot of time practising—it is a human frailty.

"So you have people in competitions, practising away very diligently working away at their technique. Then there's a fiddle player with fingers like sausages and only about a third as much ability. Yet I would listen to him play all night. Music isn't about technique. Music develops from enjoyment.

The Ninepenny Fidell

My father and mother were Irish
And I am Irish too;
I bought a wee fidil for ninepence
And that is Irish too;

I'm up in the morning early
To meet the break of day,
And to the lintwhite's piping
The many's the tunes I play!

One pleasant eve in June-time
I met a lochrie man,
His face and hands were weazen,
His height was not a span.
He boor'd me for my fidil—
"You know," says he, "like you,
My father and mother were Irish,
"And I am Irish too!"

He took my wee red fidil,
And such a tune he turned,
The Glaise' in it whispered
The Lionan in it m'urned;

Says he, "My lad, you're lucky,
"I wisht I was like you,
"You're lucky in your birth-star,
"And in your fidil too!"

He gave me back my fidil,
My fidil-stick also,
And stepping like a May-boy,
He jumped the Lear-gaidh-knowe.
I never saw him after,
Nor met his gentle kind,
But whiles I think I hear him,
A-wheening in the wind!

Joseph Campbell

The Fiddler of Dooney

When I play on my fiddle in Dooney,
Folk dance like a wave of the sea;
My cousin is priest in Kilvarnet,
My brother in Mocharabuiee.

I passed my brother and cousin:
They read in their books of prayer.
I read in my book of songs
I bought at the Sligo fair.

When we come at the end of time
To Peter sitting in state,
He will smile on the three old spirits,
But call me first through the gate;

For the good are always the merry,
Save by an evil chance,
And the merry love the fiddle,
And the merry love to dance:

And when the folk there spy me,
They will all come up to me,
With "Here is the fiddler of Dooney!"
And dance like a wave of the sea.

W. B. Yeats
1865-1939

"Personally I think it is a pity that some people waste their time trying to be really fancy. They have a much better chance of being impressive if the way they play makes people tap their feet. The trick is to be simple but entertaining."

Caoimhin Mac Aoidh places the recent success of Donegal fiddling at the door of an organization formed to promote it—Cairdeas na bhFidileiri, of which he is registrar. "Since the mid-1980s Cairdeas has had a strong development and education policy. There is an army of incredible players now, both mature and young, in the county."

The preservation of the Donegal fiddling style until the second half of the twentieth century has much to do with the geographic position of the county, tucked away as it is in the north. "Historically people either never left the county or they left the country. They did one or the other. They certainly did not circulate with the rest of Ireland. And people never came here because of its proximity to Northern Ireland."

Fiddle players have always been competitive with one another in Donegal but are not out to win converts all over the country. "The biggest priority is to play music, play it well and have fun."

That groups like Altan make a living from playing Donegal-style music is once again the icing on the cake, as far as Mac Aoidh is concerned. "They would be desperately concerned if they were able to make wallops of money but the music was in a disastrous way at home. Cairdeas is a significant priority for them.

"The music will not develop without education. Even people who seem up to their neck in commercial ventures haven't missed that in Donegal there is probably the highest concentration of fiddle teachers in Ireland. Donegal music has a natural and real importance to the people. It has a currency, a value. People share it, people spread it."

To make violins Rab Cherry uses spruce for the front, while the rest is made of maple. It takes between four and six months to complete a violin, which is almost entirely hand-crafted.

Below: *Fiddlers in Ireland may be any age, sex, or hue as this scene from Buckley's pub in Killarney illustrates. All good players are welcome at a session.*

ipes

Chaucer once said that sound was nothing but broken air. And there is no more striking way to break the air than with the pipes.

Bagpipes appear to have had a noble, if notorious, heritage. Greek philosopher Dio Chrysostom (born 40 A.D.) insisted that the Emperor Nero could "play the pipes both by means of his lips and by tucking a skin beneath his armpits." Some may claim his musical tastes were entirely in keeping with his cruel and mad ways. Those acquainted with competent bagpipe playing would beg to differ.

Rev. Dr. Campbell, Chancellor of Clogher, in 1775 wrote of his joy at a hearing pipers when he visited a house in Tipperary. "Here we are at meals, even on Sunday, regaled with the bagpipe, which, to my uncultivated ear, is not an instrument so unpleasant as the players of Italian music represent it."

Bagpipes were played 3,000 years ago in Syria. Later, they were adopted by the Romans to herald battles. As the all-conquering Romans spread across Europe, so bagpipes went with them.

The stirring sound of the pipes has long been a feature of Irish history. In fact two different types of pipes have played their part in Ireland's musical past, although the details about both are hazy. The distinction between the pair is that one was blown in the same way as the Scottish bagpipes while the other was filled by air with under-arm bellows.

The older of the pair appears to be the Scottish-style bagpipes, or *Piob mor* (warpipes), which warranted a mention in Gaelic literature of the fifth century. The Irish contingent at the battle of Crecy in France in 1346 marched to the sound of the pipes. By the fifteenth century pipes had been immortalized in a wood carving at Woodstock Castle in Co. Kilkenny. In the sixteenth century players of the Irish warpipes

were preserved for posterity in picture form by the artist Albrecht Dürer. A close cousin of the Scottish bagpipes, the Irish variety has one tenor drone while the Highland types have two.

One commentator, Stanihurst, leaves us this report of the Irish warpipes, dated 1584:

"The Irish, likewise, instead of the trumpet, make use of a wooden pipe of the most ingenious structure, to which is joined a leather bag, very closely bound with bands. A pipe is inserted in the side of this skin, through which the piper, with his swollen neck and puffed-up cheeks, blows in the same manner as we do through a tube.

"The skin, being thus filled with air, begins to swell, and the player presses against it with his arm; thus a loud and shrill sound is produced through two wooden pipes of different lengths. In addition to these there is yet a fourth pipe, perforated in different places, which the player so regulates by the dexterity of his fingers in the shutting and opening of the holes, that he can cause the upper pipes to send forth either a loud or a low sound at pleasure."

An old proverb declares that a dozen Highlanders and a bagpipe make a rebellion. So it was in Ireland, where pipers, together with harpers, would accompany soldiers into battle, urging them on to greater heroism to the throb of a nationalist theme-tune.

Bagpipes had been the instruments of kings. Henry VIII had five sets and James I was known for his skills on the pipes. However, the English planters recognized the inspirational power of the pipers at the time—and outlawed them. As Ireland lost all its armies, so the warpipes lost their raison d'être.

As the warpipes fell from grace in the middle of the eighteenth century when English repression was rife, so the quieter Uilleann pipes became eminent. Uilleann (pronounced "illyun") is derived from the old Irish name for elbow. It seems certain that Shakespeare was referring to the Uilleann pipes when he wrote of "woollen bagpipes" in *King John*, in a naive mistranslation of the word. In any event Uilleann went on to be anglicized as "union"—or perhaps the original English term was made into something altogether more Irish! Yet another term for them is the Cuisle pipes. Sometimes they were known as the Irish organ or North Country organ.

No one is sure exactly who developed the Uilleann pipes, but its two-octave range put it head-and-shoulders above its rival, the bagpipes in an era when music was becoming more complex. Along with the fiddle, the Uilleann pipes became the most popular instrument of the eighteenth century.

Composer John O'Keeffe wrote this illuminating description of the Uilleann pipes in around 1760:

"The Irish pipes have a small bellows under the left arm and a bag covered with crimson silk

The Piper and the Puca

In the old times there was a half fool living in Dunmore, in County Galway, and though he was excessively fond of music, he was unable to learn more than one tune, and that was the "Black Rogue." He used to get a good deal of money from the gentlemen, for they used to get sport out of him. One night the Piper was coming home from a house where there had been a dance and he was half drunk. When he came up to a little bridge that was by his mother's house, he squeezed the pipes on, and began playing the "Black Rogue." The Pu'ca came behind him, and flung him on his own back. There were long horns on the Pu'ca, and the Piper got a good grip of them, and then he said:

"Destruction on you, you nasty beast; let me home. I have a tenpenny-piece in my pocket for my mother, and she wants snuff."

"Never mind your mother," said the Pu'ca, "but keep your hold. If you fall, you will break your neck and your pipes." Then the Pu'ca said to him, "Play up for me the "Shan Van Vocht."

"I don't know it," said the Piper.

Never mind whether you do or you don't," said the Pu'ca. "Play up, and I'll make you know."

The Piper put wind in his bag, and he played such music as made himself wonder.

"Upon my word, you're a fine music-master," says the Piper, then; "but tell me where you're for bringing me."

There's a great feast in the house of the Banshee, on the top of Croagh Patric, tonight," says the Pu'ca, "and I'm for bringing you there to play music, and, take my word, you'll get the price of your trouble."

"By my word, you'll save me a journey, then," says the Piper, "for Father William put a journey to Croagh Patric on me because I stole the white gander from him last Martinmas.

The Pu'ca rushed him across hills and bogs and rough places, till he brought him to the top of Croagh Patric.

Then the Pu'ca struck three blows with his foot, and a great door opened, and they passed in together into a fine room.

The Piper saw a golden table in the middle of the room, and hundreds of old women sitting round about it.

The old women rose up, and said, "A hundred thousand welcomes to you, you Pu'ca of November. Who is this you have with you?"

"The best Piper in Ireland," says the Pu'ca.

One of the old women struck a blow on the ground, and a door opened in the side of the wall, and what should the Piper see coming out but the white gander which he had stolen from Father William.

"By my conscience, then," says the Piper, "myself and my mother ate every taste of that gander, besides only one wing, and I gave that to Red Mary, and it's she told the priest I stole his gander."

The gander cleaned the table, and carried it away, and the Pu'ca said, Play up music for these ladies."

The Piper played up, and the old women began dancing, and they were dancing till they were tired. Then the Pu'ca said to pay the Piper, and every old woman drew out a gold piece and gave it to him.

"By the tooth of Patric," says he, "I'm as rich as the son of a lord."

"Come with me," says the Pu'ca, "and I'll bring you home."

They went out then, and just as he was going to ride on the Pu'ca, the gander came up to him and gave him a new set of pipes.

The Pu'ca was not long until he brought him to Dunmore, and he threw the Piper off at the little bridge, and then he told him to go home, and says to him, "You have two things now that you never had before—you have sense and music." The Piper went home, and he knocked at his mother's door, saying, "Let me in, I'm as rich as a lord, and I'm the best Piper in Ireland."

"You're drunk," says the mother.

"No, indeed," says the Piper, "I haven't drunk a drop." The mother let him in, and he gave her the gold pieces, and "Wait now," says he, "till you hear the music I'll play."

He buckled on the pipes, but instead of music there came a sound as if all the geese and ganders in Ireland were screeching together. He wakened the neighbours, and they were all mocking him, until he put on the old pipes, and then he played melodious music for them; and later he told them all he had gone through that night.

The next morning, when his mother went to look at the gold pieces, there was nothing there but the leaves of a plant. The piper went to the priest and told him his story, but the priest would not believe a word from him, until he put the pipes on him, and then the screeching of the ganders and the geese began.

"Leave my sight, you thief," says the priest.

But nothing would do the Piper till he put the old pipes on him to show the priest that his story was true.

He buckled on the old pipes, and he played melodious music, and from that day till the day of his death there was never a Piper in the county Galway was as good as he was.

DOUGLAS HYDE.

under the right arm. From these passes a small leather tube of communication for the wind to reach, first, from the bellows to the bag, as both are pressed by the elbow; and from this tube another small one conveys the wind to the several pipes. That on which the fingers move is called the chanter or treble. There are three other pipes which hang over the wrist. The longest of them is called the drone or bass."

Players were now often referred to as "gentleman pipers," respected members of the community—for the gentry could indulge in a passion for music with exquisitely turned out pipes of mahogany and crushed velvet garnished with silver and ivory. Lesser folk were nevertheless not excluded. They turned to locally available woods and hemp to fashion their pipes.

Many turned their hands to composing, producing lively jigs and reels for an appreciative audience. In France the instrument's equivalent was the musette, highly fashionable during the reign of Louis XIV.

Once again it provided gainful employment for the blind. One of the most noted Irish pipe makers was William Kennedy of Tandragee, Co. Armagh, blind from the age of four. After an apprenticeship with a pipe player, Kennedy began repairing and ended up making sets of pipes. He developed the chanter keys allowing them to play sharps and flats. Several sets made by his hands still survive and one was played in 1996 at the piping festival held annually in his honor in Drumsill, Co. Armagh. Another sightless piper, William Talbot, born when Kennedy was 15, added a further two regulators to the Uilleann pipes.

Given the era, it is unsurprising to discover that no music was ever written down and no classes held in the art of piping. Tunes and skills

Below: *Leo Rickard and Martin Nolan, among the skill-saviors at Na Píobairí Uilleann, make fine music together.*

were passed on orally. The first book of bagpipe tunes ever to appear was produced during 1784.

In 1770 O'Keeffe wrote the following description of "Piper" MacDonnell.

"MacDonnell, the famous Irish piper, lived in great style—two houses, servants, hunters etc. His pipes were small and of ivory, tipped with silver and gold. You scarcely saw his fingers move, and all his attitudes, while playing, were steady and quiet, and his face composed."

As anti-Catholic measures were stepped up in Ireland in the first half of the eighteenth century it was not unknown for priests and bishops to disguise themselves as pipers and enjoy the freedom the musicians knew in order to travel unharried and continue their ministering.

Indeed, when he visited Dublin in 1821, English monarch George IV was so impressed with piper Edward Keating Hyland he ordered a new set of pipes for the musician, at a cost of 50 guineas. Hyland, who died in 1845, was blind from the age of fifteen.

In America, during the nineteenth century, Uilleann pipes were modernized by the Irish-born Taylor brothers in order to produce a greater sound.

Once again, hardships at the end of the nineteenth century forced pipers in Ireland to abandon their instruments as they battled simply to survive. By the beginning of the twentieth century the last remaining pipers were destitute.

The Uilleann pipes were the subject of a revival in the 1960s. At this time few people were playing them and only a handful of makers were in business.

Right: *Ronnie Wathen and, below, Pat Mitchell are intent on getting the best from their Uilleann pipes.*

In 1968 a Society of Pipers known as *Na Píobairí Uilleann* (The Uilleann Pipers) was founded by musicians with the express aim to perpetuate piping, particularly among the young. Their teaching program was a huge success. Within thirty years demand had risen so much that the number of pipe makers had increased to at least forty throughout the world.

One of the most famous pipers of the century was Willie Clancy (1918-73). Born near Miltown Malbay in Co. Clare, Willie was influenced by the music of Garrett Barry, a legendary blind piper who died in 1900, years before Clancy was even born, but whose music stayed very much alive in the locality.

Willie was twenty when he got hold of his first set of pipes. As a trained carpenter he worked for a while in Dublin and London before returning to Miltown Malbay in 1957.

His pipe-playing remained the mainstay of his life, however, and he became a founder member

of Na Píobairí Uilleann. He aspired to be a pipe maker but died before he fully mastered the skills.

A set of pipes has five components: bellows, beg, chanter, drones and regulator. The bag is held under one arm while the bellows is under the other. The chanter, with its range of two octaves, is the instrument of melody. The drones, meanwhile, are self-explanatory. They provide a base, baritone or tenor drone as background to the melody. Regulators are keyed chanters. There are usually three on a full set of pipes, providing an accompanying chord. Charles Roberts, of Glencar, Co. Sligo, has made and repaired pipes for thirty years. He has taken orders from countries as diverse as Argentina, Australia, Finland, New Zealand, and America. At the height of the war there he even received a request for pipes from Croatia.

It takes two or three years to produce a set of pipes. Each piece is hand-made to individual specification and the sets are then slowly assembled. Recently Roberts has had a request from Texas for a five-regulator set of pipes which could take up to five years to complete. His one concession to modern machinery is a lathe. The rest of his work is done with hand-held tools.

The high cost, at least $3,500, reflects the painstaking workmanship that goes into each set, and profits are not vast. "We do it for love. All makers are the same. If you didn't do it for love you wouldn't do it at all," explains Northumbrian-born Roberts.

He has restored two sets dating from 1890 but in piping terms that is hardly old. The most historic to pass through his hands was a William Kennedy set made in 1760.

Today's makers use much the same materials as those of years ago. This means that even the oldest sets can be rejuvenated into playing order. The only material that is now not used is ivory which was originally solely for decoration.

Roberts estimates that it takes five years for someone with musical skills to become adept at playing the pipes. Others put the figure at seven years. Seamus Ennis, a renowned piper of the twentieth century, stuck by the traditional view that it took seven years of practice and a further seven years of playing to make a piper. And even then the learning curve continues.

"The instruments are better now than they have ever been as there are more people who can repair and maintain them," says Roberts. He is sure that the present success story surrounding the Uilleann pipes lies in its flexibility.

As he points out, many cultures around the globe have their equivalent native pipes, including France, Spain, and Estonia. Most of them closely resemble bagpipes rather than Uilleann pipes and their players sometimes seek an alternative which helps to explain the popularity of the Irish pipes abroad.

"Uilleann pipes are less demanding than bagpipes which are quite physical. There are two octaves on the Uilleann pipes which makes it more appropriate for accompanied music. These days people are more able to teach themselves with so many video tape or audio tape tutors available."

Roberts has two workshops, one at his home and the other in a Craft Village run under the auspices of the Industrial Development Authority in Donegal.

Martin Nolan, a member of NPU, has provided sensible guidance for anyone wishing to purchase some pipes:

1. Do buy from an established full-time maker.
2. Do buy, when and where possible, from a maker near you.
3. Try to establish a reasonable date of delivery that suits both yourself and the maker.
4. Ensure that the pipes are in tune and made to your satisfaction before you pay.
5. Both new and second-hand pipes should be reeded before being purchased. Some reeds need to be "played in." However, if a reed is badly out of tune there is a possibility that it is the chanter which is faulty.
6. If you intend to buy a full set from a particular maker, buy a chanter (practice set) first

and if this proves satisfactory you could safely proceed with the rest.

7. Know exactly what you want before you order. It is no good changing your mind about pitch and other details when the pipes are half made.

8. Check bellows and bag for leaks and porousness, keys for stiffness and side play, and of course, key leaks.

9. Try to see other pipers who play similar sets and ask their opinion. You could ask the maker for a list of satisfied customers.

10. Be prepared for on-going repairs and general upkeep such as re-hemping the chanter top, regulator tops and drones. Key springs can become soft and may easily be re-sprung.

Right: Padraig MacMathuna plays his pipes. Those at traditional music sessions have the advantage over band pipers for at least they can remain seated.

${\frak T}$in Whistle

A simple instrument, akin to the recorder, the tin whistle is a light, metallic cylinder or cone, with finger holes. It has been in use for at least 200 years. Before that the bone whistle was widely played. Although tin whistles were used in America, England, and Scotland, it is to Irish music that they have become most closely identified.

Musically, it is surprisingly versatile. It is easily available and not expensive, nor is it terribly hard to master. Also it is simple to transport. Hence it is an ideal beginner's instrument.

Michael Whyte is a tin whistle maker in Ennis, Co. Clare. "The tin whistle is a cheap instrument but you can get great music from it. It is popular with tourists as well because it is an inexpensive souvenir but one that has some purpose and value," he explains.

When he began making tin whistles at the start of the 1980s he was among the first in Ireland to do so. Until then whistles had been imported from England. When interest in traditional music was sparse during the era of the showbands, little heed was paid to the apparently insignificant tin whistle or fipple flute as it is sometimes known. Today, it is something of a mainstay of an Irish session and demand for Irish whistles is soaring.

Below: *A woman plays the tin whistle to accompany an accordian player. Its versatility as an instrument has made it more popular today than ever before.*

Right: *A selection of tin whistles. Proficient players all have their favorites.*

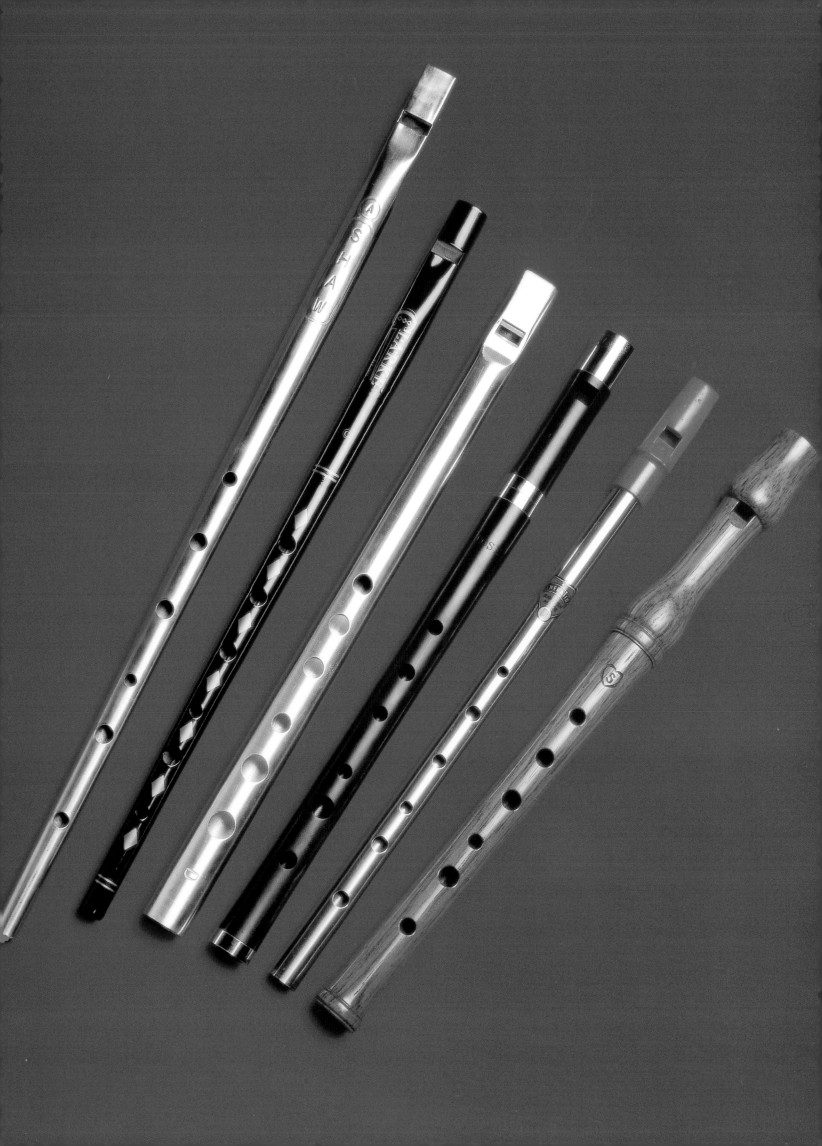

"Once you have a whistle pitched in the key of D you can play with any instrument," says Whyte. "A good whistle player can do a lot of great musical variations."

To make whistles he has to import brass tubing from Germany. While tubes made from alternative metals and alloys are available elsewhere brass is the preferred choice.

The six holes are created with a precision punch tool. Plastic, for the mouthpieces, which he buys from England, goes through an injection molding machine. It is then up to Whyte to assemble the whistle, polish, and lacquer it. The finished product costs little more than a pint of Guinness—and it should last a lifetime. While the mouthpiece may become battered or damaged, the body rarely does. Whyte will happily replace mouthpieces and reburnish the bodies to keep an ailing whistle in the business of making music.

"I like the sound of a tin whistle," admits Whyte. "You have a higher and lower octave so you can play high pitched or softly. Only if the mouthpiece is damaged do you get a fuzzy sound. It can usually be trimmed into working order."

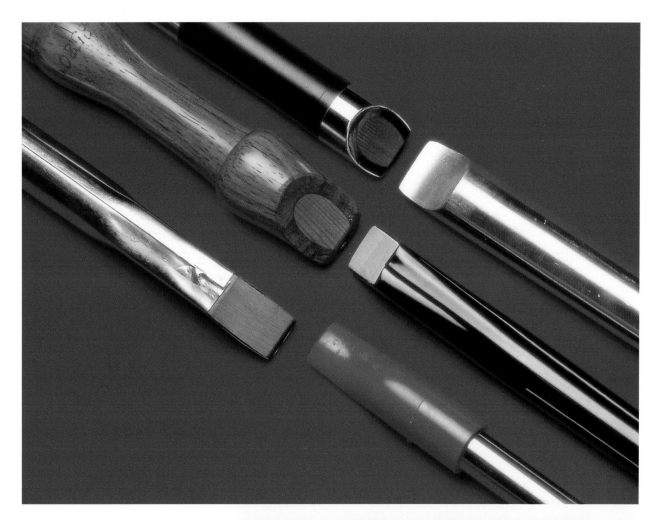

Left: *Tin whistles have an astonishing range. Brass is the preferred material for the body. Here are various examples— above left is a soprano Overton flageolet; at left is a Chieftain aluminum alloy version.*

Above: *The most likely part of a tin whistle to suffer damage is the mouthpiece. Makers like Michael Whyte are happy to carry out running repairs to keep the sound sweet.*

Right: *Once known as a "penny" whistle, this instrument is more than just a stepping stone to the flute. It has its own character and has earned its place in the Irish traditional music band on merit.*

 lute

The flute in primitive form has existed for centuries, originally emerging from the civilization of central Asia to spread, slowly but surely, through Europe, where it vied for popularity with the recorder.

Aristotle (384–322 B.C.) remained unconvinced of its benefits. "The flute is not an instrument which has a good moral effect; it is too exciting," he noted.

But Henry VIII was a fan. His biographer, Edward Halle who died in 1547, wrote that, soon after coming to the throne, Henry would enjoy these pursuits at Windsor daily: "shotying, singing, daunsyng, wrastelyng, casting of the barre, plaiyng at the recorders, flute, virginals and in settyng of songes, makyng of ballettes and did set in goodly masses, every of them fyve partes which were song oftentimes in hys chapel and afterwardes in diverse other places."

His flutes were made of wood or glass and embellished with ivory, silver or gold.

In this age the design was basic, with just six fingerholes and no thumbhole. It was little more than a fife, a shrill, small flute used to accompany drum music. As such its music was not always pleasing, as Shylock reveals in Shakespeare's *Merchant of Venice* when he recalls: "The vile squeaking of the wry-necked fife."

Consequently, the flute was subject of a range of improvements. By 1650 it was in three parts

Below: Flute players in an orchestra produce a smooth sound. In the playing of traditional Irish music breathing is altogether more apparent and provides emphasis or punctuation to phrases.

Right: Metal flutes after the style of Theobald Boehm are the choice of classical musicians. Traditional players prefer wood for its distinctive sound qualities.

and was superior in sound and application to the recorder. Still it was not the instrument we recognize today.

For this we have to thank Theobald Boehm (1794–1881), a German flautist who preferred the music created by larger holes and modified his flute accordingly. It was his changes that in 1844 prompted composer Hector Berlioz (1803–1869) to declare that the flute "for a long time so imperfect in many respects, has now achieved such perfection and evenness of tone that no further improvement remains to be desired."

He was reckoning without Boehm, whose next design, with padded lids to cover the air holes which were out of reach, made a sensational debut at London's Great Exhibition of 1851. Also, his preferred material was now silver. The design has been tweaked since then but

Right: The wooden flute is often the next instrument chosen by children who have mastered the tin whistle.

Below: Shipyard workers or factory hands, like these from Belfast, used to pool their talents and form a flute band, taking pleasure in the music they produced.

most flutes played in the world emanate from the design by Boehm.

The design and, most essentially, the choice of construction material made popular by Boehm is not favored by the flautists playing Irish traditional music, however.

It is generally felt among musicians of Celtic stock that wooden flutes of the simple system, with just six open finger holes, generate a more appropriate sound, frequently described as "breathier." Usually musicians choose to block the side keys as these are a facility rarely called upon in this brand of music.

For years the international advances in flute technology were supremely beneficial for those in pursuit of Irish traditional music. Wooden flutes were cast off by the wealthy for the new metal variety and were freely, cheaply available. It is probable that this kind of flute made its way to Ireland in the hands of the seasonal workers returning home from England. Marching bands, traditionally begun by the Temperance Movement after the 1830s, opted for the wooden flute too, perhaps for the same reason.

When the second-hand option began to dry up—particularly during the revival of Irish music—manufacture of wooden flutes began again in earnest.

odhrán

Percussion is an age-old method not only of making music but of making yourself heard. Herein lies the difficulty facing the ever-increasing number of Bodhrán players today. It is a great temptation to start banging away on the Bodhrán, to the ruination of the sounds being produced by other musicians. The Gaelic word for deaf is "bodhar," yet inexperienced players often fail to heed that subtle warning. The Bodhrán becomes deafening and its reputation takes a nosedive—so much so that Seamus Ennis was prompted to remark that the best way to play a Bodhrán was with a penknife. Another cruel critic once remarked that a Bodhrán was often a ring of beechwood separating a dead goat from a drunk skunk. One American, who was less than impressed, wrote that Bodhrán playing was "a goat's membrane being crudely assaulted by a no-brain." That the most basic of instruments can prompt such vitriol remains surprising.

A Bodhrán (pronounced bow-rawn) is a one-sided drum spanning about eighteen inches across, its skin usually made of goat's hide although some of today's alternatives have inexpensive, durable plastic heads. Goatskin is favoured by Bodhrán makers because it is unusually stretchy. The growing popularity of the Bodhrán has even sparked a scare among animal

Below: *The Bodhrán, a shallow, single-sided drum pictured here with a Celtic-style design on its face, has frequently been criticized for providing noisy, tuneless accompaniment.*

Right: *In capable hands the Bodhrán issues an irresistible beat, adding a further dimension to traditional music. Its champion was the traditional music revivalist Seán Ó'Riada.*

lovers in Ireland who fear that feral animals are disappearing from the hillsides in order to satisfy a new-found demand for goatskin. Alternatives used across the world include the skin of sheep, greyhounds, donkeys, reindeer, calf, ostrich, seal and buffalo.

The exact process of manufacture remains something of a trade secret. But the fact that the skins are treated in a mix of lime sulphate for up to ten days is in the public domain. This softens and smooths them as the hairs and the fatty tissues disintegrate. Additionally, the skins may even be buried in manure to continue the process. Rumors abound that makers would fall back on the well-matured contents of their chamber pots to achieve the right result.

When the skin is deemed suitably malleable it is stretched over frames in a heat chamber. Then it is time to apply the skins to wooden rims, generally made from beech, birch or ash. Makers once put crossbars into their frames to keep them rigid. This was when green woods were used for the rim and these were likely to warp. More recently crossbars are in danger of becoming obsolete—although they remain helpful additions for the beginner.

The Bodhrán was once known only in its native south-west corner of Ireland. Historically it was used in battle or during parades to do no more than bang out a beat. When it was not being brandished for these purposes it was likely to be re-employed as a grain tray.

It was brought out of obscurity by Seán Ó'Riada, who incorporated it into musical arrangements by groups such as the Chieftains.

The standard diameter of a Bodhrán is eighteeninches although they can range from a skimpy fifteen inches to twenty-two inches or more. Latest modifications allow for the Bodhrán to be tuned with tuning screws which can considerably adjust the sound quality.

To sound the Bodhrán you need a beater (aka a cipin, a tipper, a stick). Each may vary from the next in length, weight and shape. Beginners may want to sample different sorts to discover the one which suits them best. Flexibility in the wrist action is what counts. Those starting out should remember that slack drum heads are heavy work for the swivelling hand.

Malachy Kearns, thought to be the first full time Bodhrán maker in Ireland, is probably the best known Bodhrán maker in the world. His reputation has spread not only because of the quality of his hand-crafted drums with Celtic artwork painstakingly daubed on the face, but also through his web page on the Internet. The old world meets the new at his workshops in the grounds of a sixteenth century Franciscan monastery in Roundstone, Co. Galway.

The genial Kearns recalls the first time he saw and heard a Bodhrán:

"I was about eight years old. I can remember the hair standing up on the back of my neck!

"My father brought me to a family funeral in Donegal. It was away up in the north of Donegal somewhere near Crolly and this would have been in the late 1950s.

"We buried the man. I remember it was a cold afternoon too and afterwards the men adjourned to a pub in the village and, like a million boys of my age before and since, I was stuffed to the tonsils with orange squash and lemonade while the grown ups drank fiery glasses of whiskey and big black pints of porter. There was a fireplace with an open fire and I remember sitting beside it, late in the evening bored and stupefied with fizzy drinks and adult talking.

"Then there was a bit of excitement at the door of the bar and who came in but the legendary fiddle player Johnny Doherty, a man whose name is still spoken with near reverence by Irish musicians everywhere. He was thin and hardy, and he had his fiddle, I think, in a green velvet sack instead of a timber case. He had small, quick hands and a very quiet way about him. There was another man with him and he had a sack with him too, a jute one this time, and when he left it down on the floor beside me, carefully, I heard it make a boomy kind of noise.

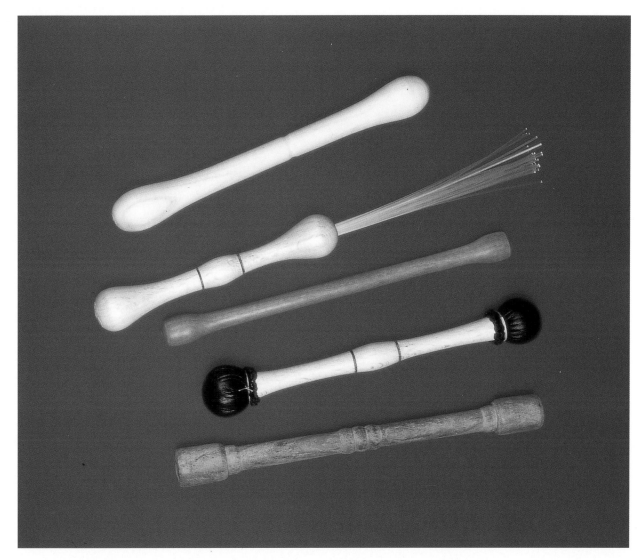

Above: *A selection of Bodhrán beaters.*

Below left: *Bodhrán, fiddle, and stout—perfect companions.*

"Johnny Doherty, still regarded as the prince of Donegal fiddlers, was a master musician who was also a semi-traveler. He moved all around Donegal at different times of the year staying and playing in selected houses for weeks and months at a time. It was a great honor to have him stay and make his music under your roof. People came from everywhere just to hear him play.

"Even as a child I knew there was something special about him when he began to play in that pub. He was sitting in the chair opposite me, swaying a bit in the gale of his own jigs and reels, his eyes empty and full in his face at the same time, as if they were seeing the music in some strange way, and nothing else. The men that were standing listening and sitting listening were silent except to say 'Good Man Johnny' now and again, and they even forgot that they had drinks in their hands. It was beautiful stuff.

"But after a while it was even better because the other man that was with Johnny Doherty . . . and somebody told me he was a real traveler . . .

he eventually took the first Bodhrán I ever saw out of the jute bag. He warmed it by the fire, rubbing it now and again so that it muttered and grumbled almost, and then, without any beater . . . . he began to play. And it was absolutely mighty."

His love affair with the Bodhrán is infectious. Consequently, his drums have traveled far and wide. They have gone all over the world in the hands of visitors impressed by his work at Roundstone. They have been on tour with folk icon Christy Moore, to football stadia in the hands of Irish soccer fans and on tour with the phenomenal show *Riverdance*.

Often his products bear testimony to his wife Anne's love of heraldry, decorated by a coat of arms. Another tell-tale sign of his work is the way the skins on the Bodhrán are stuck down rather

than tacked. Malachy Kearns prefers to glue the hide in place so it cannot rip off and has developed his own strong adhesive. He has a monthly "goat day" when suppliers visit his workshop

"If my people of the goats share common traits, they are that they are all colorful, that they love Irish music, and in many cases are musicians themselves and also that they all have a great love for the environment and especially for the wiry goats whose skins, when the animals have finished their tenancy of them, come down to me along the twisty road to Roundstone . . .

"For the goats whose hides are the commerce of my skin days, with all their color and excitement, it is surely the time of the Phoenix. They rise again."

Malachy struggles to put into words the feeling that the Bodhrán inspires.

"The first time your run your fingers over the head of a new Bodhrán is like bringing something to life.

"Sometimes it's almost as if you can hear the robin that sang in the beech tree, or the wind that blew through it on some summery day when its roots were searching down deep in Mother Earth for all the sixty gallons of water that a beech tree needs to keep it alive each day of its prime growing.

"Or the breathing of a man that was maybe a bit drunk coming home late, and needed to lean against it for a while. Staggering.

"Or, out of the goatskin itself, the sense of wild freedom, the sense of the paganism of nature, of the freshest of fresh air up amongst the peaks where men don't go.

"The Bodhrán beat . . . is truly the pulse of Irish music and our rich outpouring of our unmatch reservoir of folk music is indeed the blood in the arteries of our culture.

"To be at the center of that, each time I run my fingers across a new Bodhrán, as yet unplayed, but already silently singing its wild tunes, is to be in a very special and very spiritually rewarding place."

Left: *Bodhráns might bear a variety of insignia, hand painted on to the smooth, tight goat-skin. Thus each Bodhrán will sound different and may look different too.*

Below: *The crosspiece makes an ideal "handle" for those learning to play.*

Playing the Bodhrán

1. Sit upright holding the crosspiece of the drum and resting the rim against your left shoulder and left leg. (The position is reversed for left-handed people.)

2. With the right hand take the stick and hold it in the middle as if it were a pen. Strike the skin with the "writing" end, propelling the stick through a right-angle.

3. Mentally divide the drum like a clock, 12, 9, 6, and 3 o'clock. There are two areas on which to make a start. I have suggested two areas because you may feel comfortable with one or the other to practice on.
a) The 9 o'clock area, or back end of the drum. Point beater end to nine, bring stick down and strike at 7.30 and allow stick to follow through past 6 towards 5. This is the downward stroke. The upward stroke follows immediately afterwards, bringing the stick back from 5, hitting once again at 7.30 and following through past 9.
b) The 3 o'clock area or front end of the drum. Point beater at 12, bring stick down and strike at 3, follow through to five and reverse for the up stroke.

REMEMBER: when striking the beat you must hit the skin towards the middle, not at the edge.

4. Loosen the wrist, balance the stick, keep the shoulder straight.

5. Practice, practice, practice.

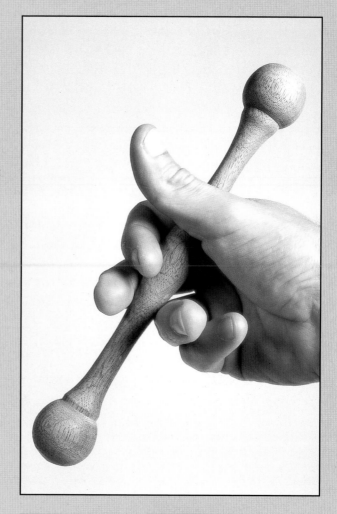

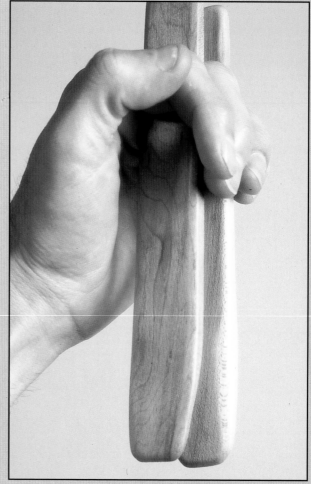

Above right: *The correct position to hold the Bodhrán beater.*

Right: *The bones, another Irish traditional instrument.*

Far right: *How to hold and play a Bodhrán.*

Concertina

The concertina came into existence in 1844 when Charles Wheatstone, creator of the mouth-blown brass-reeded symphonium, experimented with bellows. The symphonium was a forerunner of the harmonica but had buttons to control the outlet of air. In its new life as a concertina it was hand held with the fingers of each hand playing notes by depressing studs. The shape was distinctively hexagonal. Tchaikovsky used four concertinas in his second orchestral suite. Its popularity was widespread in the last half of the nineteenth century but it has since been confined to folk music.

Right and Below: A concertina sounds when air is squeezed from the bellows which lie between the handles. By depressing different buttons with the fingers the note is changed. This is an Ashdown thirty-key Anglo, which differs from an English concertina in the fact that each button produces a different note on the push and draw of the bellows.

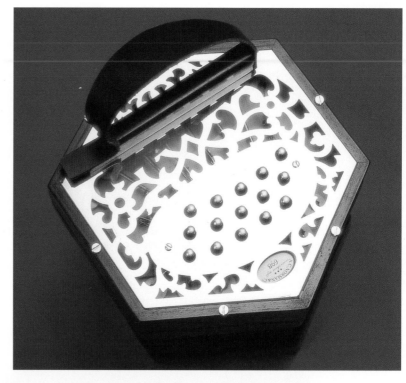

Above: *Two musicians—clearly unused to being in the spotlight—are captured in action in a pub in Lisdoonvarna, Co. Clare, on August 1, 1989.*

Left: *Concertinas are lightweight and compact, controlled by the touch of a button.*

Accordion

Also related to the harmonica, the accordion was conceived in 1821 when German instrument maker Friedrich Buschmann modified a mouth-blown aura with bellows. Just eight years later, Cyrillus Demian of Vienna unveiled his box-shaped accordion with its finger buttons, the left playing chords and the right the melody. Later the Italian Mariano Dallape used piano keys to replace the right-hand buttons and the piano-accordion was born. The Spanish composer Roberto Gerhard (1896–1970) experimented with the sound and wrote his "Concerto" for eight instruments, including the accordion. During the nineteenth century the accordion found its way to Ireland, probably in the fists of seasonal workers, and became the ideal accompaniment for set dances.

Above: *An accordion player from Monkstown Co. Dublin, in action, his fingers capable of flying over the keys.*

Left: *Accordions have been with us for more than 170 years. Some models have an impressive heritage behind them. This is an Italian melodian made by Mengascini.*

Right: *Festivals like this one are held across Ireland and have done much to promote the image of Irish traditional music.*

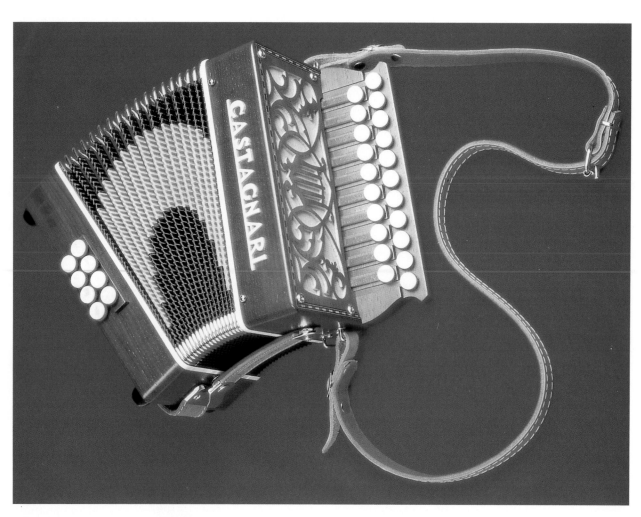

Above left and Left: *Accordions come in various shapes and sizes. Some have piano keys while other retain buttons as per the original design. However, the principle behind them—of central bellows and air being forced through holes of different sizes—remains the same.*

Above: *A piano accordion, where a keyboard replaces the buttons. This is made by the famous manufacturer Paolo Soprani from Castelfidardo.*

Sometimes knows as the squeeze box, otherwise just the box. Joe Cooley and Joe Burke are among the best known box players on the Irish traditional music scene.

Eighty years ago the box was generally thought to be an unwelcome intruder into the Irish traditional music scene.

Michael Coleman, the renowned Irish fiddler, was once asked for a dollar as a contribution for a box-player's funeral. He dug deep. "Here's two dollars," he quipped. "Bury two of them."

Bouzouki

The bouzouki is a stringed instrument commonly found in European folk music. It is a newcomer to the Irish traditional music scene, emerging in the past 30 years. Johnny Moynihan, of the Dublin group Sweeney's Men, as well as Andy Irvine and Alec Finn are the musicians widely credited with the innovation of using bouzoukis. Thanks to the revival in Irish traditional music, interest in this instrument has mushroomed.

Now, the Irish bouzouki has developed as an instrument in its own right, subtly differing from its Greek parent.

Martin Faherty is an Irish bouzouki maker at the Shandon Craft Centre in Cork and explains the new breed.

"The Greek bouzouki has a round back like a lute, lighter strings and often a longer neck, by about two frets. The Greeks play much faster in trills. It is not used as an accompanying instrument.

"The Irish bouzouki is flat-backed. It also has a heavier string giving it a different sound. It can be used to play tunes, as well as to accompany singing or other instruments.

"It is a unique instrument. It doesn't bear that much resemblance to the Greek bouzouki in the music that is played on it or the sound it makes."

The Irish bouzouki has four double strings, generally tuned to DADA (known, unsurprisingly, as Dada) and is played with a plectrum.

In general terms the bouzouki takes the place of the guitar in sessions. Although it was used during the revival of Irish traditional music the guitar was strongly associated with rock and pop and had not earned its stripes in other spheres; this fact sitting uncomfortably among some musicians.

Left and Right: *Bouzoukis and mandolins are often used in Irish music. The bouzouki is a newcomer to the Irish music scene. It came over from Greece in the hands of an enthusiast and quickly became incorporated into the traditional style. This is a Gibson "A" Model mandolin.*

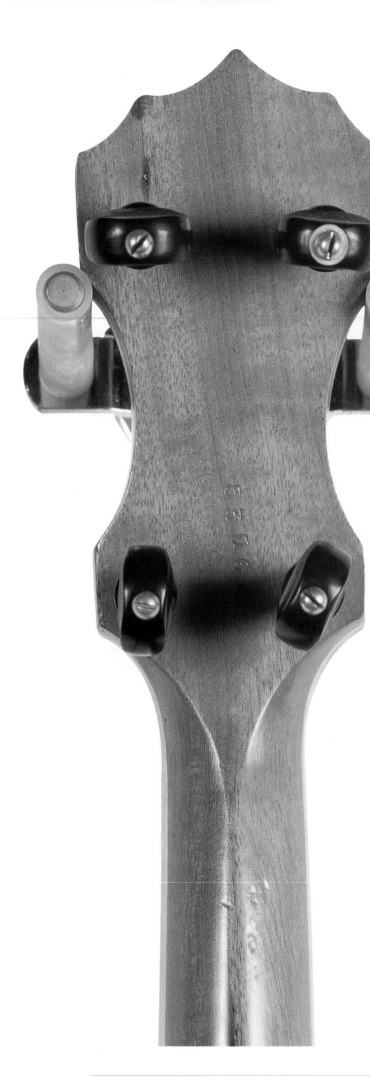

The sound quality of the bouzouki is distinctive. Said Flaherty, who plays both instruments: "It still has that Greek or Eastern flavor, an exotic sound like a sitar. When the strings are struck it gives off sounds other than the note itself, even sometimes the sound of disharmony. It is rhythmic, played with open chords and it's very often used in a similar way to a snare drum. And the sound carries better than that of the guitar. The standard of playing has risen tremendously, too."

He makes bouzoukis from the same woods used for guitar-making—Indian rosewood, mahogany, maple or walnut for the back and spruce or cedar for the front. Apart from using a band-saw to cut a large piece of wood to size Flaherty creates the instrument by hand. It takes him about two weeks to make a bouzouki.

"There is no advantage in using new technology for me. The acoustic work is done by hand, it is the only way if the finished product is to sound right for the customer. The labor involved is the most expensive part of the instrument because it is so time-consuming."

The sound of the bouzouki is equally distinct from that of the mandolin, which also has its place in Irish music.

"The mandolin is a higher-pitched instrument with a treble sound and is used more for melody. Even if you played on the higher frets of the bouzouki you would not get the mandolin sound."

The heyday of the mandolin was in the nineteenth century when mandolin bands thirty or forty strong were popular in America, Holland and Germany. In America, where mandolins were used a folk instruments and played Irish, Bluegrass and other "high lonesome" musical genres, the Gibson mark on a mandolin was deemed to be one of quality. In Europe the mandolin was adopted in classical music.

Left: *The neck of a Greek bouzouki is generally two frets longer than its Irish offspring.*

Above and Right: *A comparison between a Bouzouki (Right) and an Octave Mandola shows the strong physical similarities.*

anjo

Originally, the banjo was the instrument of the plantation slaves and was played by them in America as early as the seventeenth century. However, it is best know for its role in minstrel shows or vaudeville, the entertainment associated with America in the nineteenth and early 20th centuries. It was probably in the hands of touring US minstrels with blackened faces that the banjo first made its way to Ireland in about 1840. The phenomenal rise to fame of the Irish group the Dubliners in the 1960s is generally credited with the re-emergence of the banjo on the music scene. It has since been widely adopted by Irish musicians and it is commonly found in a traditional session. Briefly, the instrument is a round metal hoop covered with parchment on one side. It has a fretted fingerboard and three, four, five, or six strings.

Banjos are shallow, unlike the bouzouki. These days the backs are generally wooden and may be decorative.

The Collectors

Controversy over the collectors of Irish music has further muddied the waters of Irish traditional music.

Most of the musical pieces from medieval times were learned orally rather than written. This has meant that virtually nothing remained in manuscript form which could be revived by future generations.

Bunting and his contemporaries helped to bridge the gap by collecting Irish music and noting down the tunes.

To their credit, this work has left something tangible with which musicians could get to grips from an area which had, until then, been woefully neglected. Were it not for Bunting there would be little old-style harp music in existence today.

However, some musical scholars believe that collections made years ago are seriously flawed. They fear the raw edge of traditional music was sacrificed rather than saved by the likes of Bunting.

After all, Bunting did not even speak Gaelic, the very language of the songs in which he was dealing. So it is a matter of contention whether he could fully understand and appreciate their

Above: *A view of Bantry Bay from Bantry House gardens in Co. Cork. The collection of Irish airs was at first a strictly middle class pastime.*

BUNTING

Tonight at 9.15 a programme will be broadcast commemorating the work of Edward Bunting, who spent his life collecting the songs and tunes of Ireland as he heard them sung and played on the harp.

Left: *Edward Bunting (1773-1843), founder of the Irish Harp Society, was a musician and teacher credited with making the first records of Irish harp music. He was present at the Belfast Harp Festival of 1792, where he was witness to a vanishing style of harp playing. By notating what he heard he ensured its continuance, even though the demands of popular music at the time made what he produced a somewhat inaccurate record.*

Above: *Sir Charles Gavan Duffy (1816-1903) was an Irish nationalist whose "Ballad Poetry of Ireland" rapidly became a household name in Ireland. Duffy himself, meanwhile, emigrated to Australia and became its Prime Minister in 1871!*

Above right: *Douglas Hyde (1860-1949), one of Ireland's renaissance men. Not only was he a poet, philologist and historian, he was also founder of the Gaelic League, or Connradhna Gaedhilge. This was an organisation chiefly concerned with the conservation of Gaelic culture. An important work it undertook was the publication of "The Roche Collection of Irish Tradtional Music", a collection made by Neill Francis Roche between 1912 and 1927.*

Right: *Ireland is by no means the only country with a sense of the importance of its folk heritage. While Irish folk music was being recorded by the likes of Francis O'Neill and Neill Francis Roche, British composer George Butterworth (1885-1916) made a collection of English folk songs during his life.*

worth. He also imposed his own classical prejudice on the tunes, notating them in impossible keys and adding unplayable accidentals. By his own confession he made changes to the music before publishing—and arranged the scores for piano accompaniment, probably to achieve some commercial success. He almost certainly favored the respected and respectable harp above the music of the peasantry which would have been deemed unworthy of note.

Yet perhaps Bunting, who published three collections, should also be merited for beginning a tradition of collecting old songs or airs. After him came Thomas Moore and his *Irish Melodies* in 1807 which were inspired by old tunes; George Petrie and, most significantly, Francis O'Neill.

At the time of the Belfast Harp Festival Bunting (1773–1843) was nineteen years old, a church organist who had been hired to note

down the melodies of the harpers. He did so with passion, perhaps realizing the greatness which had been thrust upon him. For a golden era of traditional Irish music was drawing inexorably to a close.

Four years later he published his first collection containing sixty-six airs. In 1802, with Irish-speaking schoolmaster Patrick Lynch from Co. Down in tow, Bunting toured Munster and Connaught aiming to collect still more of the old music and not simply that written for harps.

His second volume was published in 1809 containing seventy-seven airs, while his third and last collection came in 1840 with 151 numbers.

A year later, Henry Hudson began publishing Irish tunes in *The Citizen*, a magazine published in Dublin. Within two years more than 100 had appeared in the periodical. On his death in 1889 Hudson, who began collecting Irish tunes at the age of fourteen, had amassed more than 700 tunes and an additional 100 or more of his own compositions based on folk music of the era.

Above: *John Field (1782–1837) was an Irish pianist and composer who, in 1803, moved to St. Petersburg and toured Europe from there before his death in Moscow.*

Right: *Irish-born Sir Charles Villiers Stanford (1852–1924) was a composer, conductor and organist who proved hugely influential on a generation of English composers. His music frequently reflected an abiding interest in Irish folk tunes.*

Above: *Members of the Irish Music Society gather at unveiling of a statue of poet Thomas Moore (pictured left) in 1922, 70 years after his death. His lyrics were popular among the English and endured for years but are not, strictly speaking, in the traditional style.*

Cork-born William Forde was also at work gathering musical references at the time. His area of speciality was the music of Connaught but he was hampered by financial constraints and nothing emerged as a published work.

The most eminent of the collectors of the era was Dr. George Petrie, who was born in Dublin of Scottish ancestry. A scholar of broad interests he was thoroughly absorbed by Irish music, revealing a preference for songs rather than tunes. In 1855 he published his *Ancient Music of Ireland* (one of three tomes bearing the same name by different collectors). Three further volumes of works he collected were published after his death. In 1905 Sir Charles Stanford published

Above: *Herbert Hamilton Harty (1879–1941), the Northern Irish conductor and composer, was flying the flag for Ireland in the world of classical music when the traditional scene was in the doldrums.*

the *Complete Petrie Collection* of 1,582 numbers although Petrie had in fact recorded 2,148 pieces with additional descriptive notes.

Patrick Weston Joyce (1827-1914) offered immense assistance to Petrie. After the latter's death he published his *Ancient Music of Ireland* containing 100 tunes never before seen in print. There followed a second volume in 1888 and then, in 1909, his *Old Irish Folk Music*.

Much of his inspiration for the last volume came from John Edward Pigot (1822–71) and James Goodman (1828–96) from Ventry, both of whom were prolific collectors with some 2,000 airs under their belts.

Francis O'Neill had an advantage over the rest of the famous collectors. He was born an Irishman and, more to the point, he played the music the rest could only write about.

O'Neill hailed from West Cork, emigrating at the age of 16 for a life of adventure. He was a sailor turned teacher, who finally distinguished himself in the Chicago police force. His first love, however, was Irish traditional music. As a flute player he was part of numerous sessions, met the eminent musicians of the time and also had a host of tunes already committed to memory.

O'Neill himself could not write music and relied upon a fellow policeman and fiddle player, Sgt. James O'Neill, to copy down the notes of tunes regaled by himself or other musicians. Having written it down, James O'Neill played back the tune and made modifications to the satisfaction of the contributor. The flexibility of Irish music worked against James O'Neill. A musician would play it once, repeat it, and then go through it a third time—and each version would sound different. Today, of course, a tape recorder alleviates this problem.

There are 1,850 tunes in O'Neill's *Music of Ireland*, the largest printed collection of Irish traditional tunes ever. His other most notable publication was 1001 tunes which became known simply as "The Book."

Thus the O'Neill collections are a Bible among disciples of Irish traditional music. They have even been called the savior of Irish traditional music. But they also pose dilemmas. Errors mean some of the notes are distinctly awry. There is no indication of grace notes or ornamentation, perhaps because James O'Neill, in the mold of Bunting before him, was classically trained and therefore unfamiliar with Irish traditional music in its written form. Of course, ornamentation also varies between the regions of Ireland, making the task even more unfathomable. And as Francis O'Neill once observed: "It all depends on individual taste as to which version of a tune is the most meritorious."

Soon after, O'Neill Francis Roche of Limerick made his collections on behalf of the Gaelic League. Between 1912 and 1927 he published three volumes of *The Roche Collection of Irish Traditional Music*.

Above right: *Irish-born tenor John McCormack (1884–1945) takes a bow at London's Royal Albert Hall. He did much to popularise the well-loved ballad* The Star of the County Down.

Below right: *Seán Ó'Riada, who loathed the sound of the Céilí bands when they had all but swamped the music scene in Ireland, revamped traditional music and breathed new life into an ailing art form.*

ongs

From the loins of little Ireland some mighty literary figures have been spawned: Jonathan Swift, Oscar Wilde, George Bernard Shaw, James Joyce, W. B. Yeats—to name but a handful.

But in Ireland, dextrous and lyrical use of language is by no means the preserve of the famous few. The Irish have a long-standing love of words. Brendan Behan (1923–64) was fascinated by the richness of everyday conversations even among the most humble. According to his biographer, Ulick O'Connor Behan found that: "Even their swearing was more than mere cursing; it was an orchestration of words, used musically with a sense of the rhythm of language to improve the effect of their sentences. Words choicely chosen gave them the same pleasure that others might get from food or drink."

Fortunately, such words were not only captive in the pages of books, which for so long were available to the wealthy minority alone. They were fodder for the rest of the population, too, in the form of well-loved songs. These historical reflections were handed down from generation to generation and a generous number survive.

The songs may be love songs or landscape songs, tales of suffering or derring-do, ditties or diatribes, sung in hauntingly sentimental or strikingly rebellious tones. Their language varies from velvet to acid. The themes of numerous songs reflect the troubled history of Erin.

Above: *Rifles Band, 1889.*

Right: *The banjo plays its part in the sound generated by "Blackthorn."*

Writer Donal O'Sullivan said of Irish music: "One finds in the best of these songs a beauty and tenderness beyond the ordinary; a deep and passionate sincerity; a naturalness which disdains all artifice; a feeling for poetical expression unusual in folk songs; all combined with a mellifluous assonance which makes them singable."

The lover's lament of *Donall Og* illustrates his point.

From me you've stolen East and also West
You took my past and my future too
The sun and moon, you taken them away
To take my God from me I'm most afraid.

Ballads are a mirror of social times. Many Irish songs reflect what is going on at the time of writing. Indeed, Ireland has few if any native nursery rhymes and commits most of its history to song. That continues to the present day with new songs devoted to successful Gaelic football teams, soccer stars, or national heroes being penned regularly.

Today, the identity of the vast majority of traditional or folk song-writers has been lost. By careful study of the lyrics side-by-side with the history of Ireland we can gauge the life and times of singers and song-writers.

Ireland's natural beauty has been an inspiration to many. Cliffs, mountains, shorelines, loughs, plains, and pastures are abundant, all clothed in green. Just as the aspects of nature's splendors roused poets to verse so they have provoked minstrels.

Yet for two centuries the population of Ireland migrated across the globe. Few countries have known such wholesale desertion by its population and emigration has left its mark on the country's culture.

To many the memory of Ireland's verdant landscapes loomed large in their minds long after they left. Indeed, the vast majority of those who waxed lyrically about the landscape of Ireland did so when they were absent. It was those exiled from the land they loved, and the emotions that they recorded, which are fundamental to numerous Irish traditional songs. The theme of melancholy recurs time and again.

The past joy and present sadness shines through words of the unknown writer of *Lovely Leitrim*. Here are the first and last verses:

Below: *Instruments, especially drums, have a long history not only in making music but in attracting attention of others. This band was on the march to summon voters to a speech being given by politician James M. Dillon during an Irish election campaign.*

Right: *Evening at Lough Mackno, Co. Monaghan.*

Seán-nos singing

In addition to ballads there is seán-nos or old–style singing which tends to be unaccompanied, in the Irish language and was popular in the early part of the twentieth century. Words and music are equally important in seán-nos singing. It is notable for the emotion that the singer instills into the song and the individual style or ornamentation employed. Seán-nos singing knows three main styles, those of Donegal, Connemara, and Munster. Much of this type of singing has been found in its original form among the traveling people of Ireland. For many years traveling people were without the distractions of television, radio—or even electric lights. Seán-nos singing was the perfect antidote to a gloomy evening, and many songs which no longer had currency in Irish society remained intact thanks to the travelers.

Above: *Kilkenny Castle rising from the River Nore in Kilkenny City.*

Left: *The O'Connell Bridge spanning the River Liffey in Dublin.*

Right: *Autumn comes to Killykeen Forest Park in Co. Cavan.*

Last night I had a pleasant dream,
I woke up with a smile;
I dreamt that I was back again
In dear old Erin's Isle.
I thought I saw Lough Allen's banks,
In the valleys down below,
It was my lovely Leitrim
Where the Shannon waters flow.

I've travelled far to these great lands,
From the east into the west,
But of all the islands I have seen
I love my own the best.
And if ever I return again,
There's one place I will go,
It will be lovely Leitrim, where
The Shannon waters flow.

Many must have echoed the sentiments of this tortured soul who penned *The Cliffs of Duneen.*

I have travelled far, far from my own native home,
Far away o'er the mountains, far away o'er the foam;
I've seen many sights, many places I've been,
But there's none can compare with the Cliffs of Duneen.

Above: *Although an English-speaker by birth, Seán O'Casey learned Gaelic and was a fervent supporter of the nationalist cause.*

Below: *A flute and the mighty lambeg drum heads an Orange parade in 1951. Remarkably the flute is still heard above the drum thud.*

Above: *Irish writer and nationalist Brendan Behan at the piano.*

Those who left fall, roughly speaking, into three categories. There were those without choice, sent away by the judiciary as punishment; those forced out by hardship, and, later, those who chose to leave to pursue their hopes and dreams.

Irish nationalists and criminals who escaped the noose were among those who were transported by way of punishment, first to America and, when that ended in 1775 due to the War of Independence, to Australia. Transportation to the inhospitable terrain of Australia endured for almost eighty years, until 1868.

The Fields of Athenry tells the tale of a sweetheart whose lover is dispatched on a prison ship.

She watched the last star falling
As the prison ship sailed out against the sky.
But she'll wait and hope and pray
For her love in Botany Bay
For it's lonely round the fields of Athenry.

Poverty and hunger were the driving forces for the majority who left. And the floodgates opened after the Great Famine when the potato crop failed and the population starved in their droves.

By now the land had been divided into scores of small farms. The potato, that most versatile of vegetables, was ideal both to eat and to trade with—until a devastating blight left them all rotten in the ground. For three years in the mid-1840s the crop failed. More than two thirds of the population depended on farming to live as, in Ireland, the industrial age was still some way off. Things went from bad to very much worse.

Consider the plight of little Catherine Sheehan of Bantry, who died on Boxing Day in 1846 age two, after living for days on a diet of only seaweed. She was merely one of thousands. Men, women and children collapsed by roadsides, in fields or in their homes. The skin clung to their bones, gaunt and grey.

Rural priests worked long hours, often delivering the last rites to several members of the same family as they lay destitute and starving in their remote homes. There was no spare money for clothes or fuel. As winter rolled relentlessly around, it further ravaged the inadequately covered bodies already weakened from hunger. For most there was not enough money for a coffin. The majority were buried in the rags which dressed them. Even the dogs were reduced to eating bark from the trees.

In *Old Skibbereen* an emigrant father explains to his son why he left Ireland.

Oh son! I loved my native land with energy and pride,
Till a blight came o'er my crops—my sheep, my cattle
died;
My rent and taxes were too high, I could not them
redeem,
And that's the cruel reason that I left old Skibereen.

When food ran short in the countryside, the same privations were mirrored in city life. There was accommodation in the workhouses for some, although most were so frail by the time they arrived that they soon died. And when the workhouses became overcrowded the diseases of typhus and dysentery, which so often inhabit such conditions, took hold. The very air was fetid and heavy with the stench of death. There were food riots in Dublin—although the Irish knew of old the hopelessness of protest against the British authorities.

In July 1847 the *Dublin University Magazine* published the *Song of the Famine*, which paints a powerful contemporary portrait of the sufferings which occurred.

Food! Food! Food!
Beware before you spurn,
Ere the cravings of the famishing
To loathing madness turn;
For hunger is a fearful spell,
And fearful work is done,
Where the key to many a reeking crime,
Is the curse of living on!

Home! Home! Home!
A dreary fireless hole
A miry floor and a dripping roof,
And a little straw—its whole.
Only the ashes that smolder not,
Their blaze was long ago,
And the empty space for kettle and pot,
Where once they stood in a row!

Only the naked coffin of deal,
And the little body within,
It cannot shut it out from my sight,
So hunger-bitten and thin;
I hear the small weak moan
The stare of the hungry eye,
Though my heart was full of a strange, strange joy
The moment I saw it die.

Could nothing have been done? The argument still rages today about whether the ruling English should have intervened faster and more effectively. Public works programs offered some employment, but the result was newly constructed roads that led nowhere and waterless canals.

The English government bought Indian meal in bulk from the United States, which in March 1846 sold for a penny a pound. No one realized that it lacked essential vitamins. Those who refused it, describing it as "nothing better than sawdust," were close to the mark.

Only later were soup kitchens dispatched across Ireland to distribute free food. For many the situation was, by then, hopeless. Indeed, a square meal bolted down after months of deprivation was often fatal. The inaction of the British government has lately been labeled genocide. In the context of the era this considerably overstates the case. However, in 1997 British prime minister Tony Blair was moved to apologize for the inadequacies of his predecessors. In a letter sent to a festival in Cork held to mark the famine he wrote: "Those who governed in London at the time failed their people through standing by while a crop failure turned into a massive human tragedy. That one million people should have died in what was then part of the richest and most powerful nation in the world is something that still causes pain as we reflect on it today."

The population figures of the era make sobering reading. In 1841 the census revealed the Irish population to be 8,747,588. A decade later the figure had dropped to 6,515,794—a drop of more than 2.2 million.

Not all of the "disparus" were lost to the famine. Emigration was the alternative remedy to

Right: Seán Ó'Riada split music from dance, renting apart an attachment that had lasted for centuries. He put it in the concert halls with the aim of producing a highbrow music for Ireland.

and benefits of living overseas. Land, clothing and food still cost money and the emigrants arrived with virtually none. If they won jobs they were menial ones. Women, perhaps, had better prospects as they might be taken on as servants. The Irish, widely associated with the sin of drinking to excess, soon formed an underclass. Here was another form of tyranny from which it was hard to escape.

The first verse of a folk song written in the 1870s reveals the plight of many.

I am a decent Irishman from Ballifad,
And I want a situation and I want it mighty bad.
A position I saw advertised is the thing for me says I,
But the dirty spalpeen ended with
"No Irish Need Apply."

For this reason some returned home and more would have done so if they had the money as some much-vaunted folk songs reveal.

The author of *I'll Take You Home Again Kathleen* laments the sadness that his wife endures away from her home. The final verse reads:

To that dear land beyond the sea,
My Kathleen shall again return,
And when thy old friends welcome thee,
Thy loving heart will cease to yearn,
Where laughs the little silver stream,
Beside your mother's humble cot,
And brightest rays of sunshine gleam,
There all your grief will be forgot.

It's worth noting that some struck out to the rich farming lands and made homes reminiscent of those back in Ireland. Many were Protestants, or "Scots-Irish" as the Americans know them, who traditionally had more money than their Catholic counterparts.

Remember, too, that thousands of Irish men and women overcame a long-standing loathing

Left: *Red-haired boy.*

Irish music and poetry has not remained rooted in the past. Irish pop and rock stars are among the most influential in the world. Some of them are illustrated on the following pages.

Above right: *Irish singer-songwriter and champion of the starving Bob Geldof.*

Right: *Another Irish icon, Bono of U2 during 1985 Live Aid.*

The Soldier's Song

Since 1926 the Irish national anthem has been *The Soldier's Song*, written by Peadar Kearney, uncle of Brendan Behan. He wrote it in 1907 as a march and, to this day, it sounds more becoming with the backing of a military band rather than an orchestra.

It became the theme music of the Easter Rising of 1916, with captive rebels singing it in defiance of the English prison masters.

The song ultimately outperformed two rival patriotic tunes to win the accolade of anthem status. Those were *A Nation Once Again* by Thomas Davis and *God Save Ireland*, a Fenian piece about the Manchester Martyrs.

The Soldier's Song was written in and is meant to be sung in Irish. There follows an English approximation of the words.

We'll sing a song, a Soldier's Song,
with cheering, stirring chorus;
As round our blazing fires we gather,
the starry heavens o'er us;
Impatient for tomorrow's fight,
as we await the morning's light;
Here in the quiet of the night we will chant a
*   Soldier's Song.*

(Chorus)
Soldiers are we,
whose lives are pledged to Ireland;
Some have arrived from a land overseas.
Sworn to be free,
No more our ancient fatherland shall shelter the
*   dictator or the slave*
Tonight we man the Gap of Danger,
in Erin's cause come woe or wail;
Mid cannon's roar and rifle's peal we will chant a
*   Soldier's Song.*

Right: *Michael Collins took part in the Easter Rising, was interned in Frognoch until December 1916, and stood for Sinn Fein in the 1918 election. He became Finance Minister in the in the first Irish parliament. It was Collins who signed the Anglo-Irish Treaty of 1921 which allowed the creation of Eire—he would die during the Irish Civil War in 1922 while commander of the Free State's armed forces.*

Left: *The entrance to Kilmainham Jail where the executions of a number of the Easter Rising's leaders took place, including James Connolly, who led the Irish Citizen Army in the rising and who faced the firing squad in a chair as his wounds prevented him from standing.*

Below: *Damage to Dublin caused by the rising was extensive but localized. Here is O'Connell Street Bridge, with O'Connell's monument at left.*

of Britain and emigrated there, short and long-term. After about 1830, during the Industrial Revolution, the building of canals and railways offered more jobs than the resident workforce could satisfy.

Labor was, once again, in short supply during the two world wars. Ireland, although neutral during World War II, found itself supplying factory workers and, later, manpower for rebuilding program.

Irish political history is complex and this is not the place for its dissection. However, it is impossible to even glance at Irish traditional music without making some sense of this country's troubled and tragic past.

The Introduction touched on the history of Ireland—the arrival of the Celts, conquest by the Normans, the religious bigotry of the Elizabethan Protestants, the Great Famine, and the 1916 Easter Rising. While it may seem that Irish history was a long story of rebellion, this is an oversimplification. There were, certainly, those who preached revolt against the British crown, but they were in a minority. Indeed, the Easter Rising was not well supported and almost went

Above: Van Morrison, the Irish singer-songwriter pictured here in 1986, has offered another facet to the small island's vibrant music scene.

the way of previous rebellions. It was the way that the British reacted, shooting the ringleaders out of hand, that gave the movement impetus it needed.

When it came, the independence offered by the British Government was opposed both by Republicans, who believed it offered too little, and Ulster Protestants who thought it gave away far too much. The Republican movement, Sinn Fein, declared an independent Ireland in 1919 but the turmoil that had blighted Ireland for so long then erupted into civil war between those fighting for a completely free Ireland and those who accepted partition.

A peace formula which had southern counties forming an Irish Free State while six predominantly Protestant counties in the north remained allied to Britain was finally agreed, although the fight has continued. The direct effects of Henry VIII's urgent desire for divorce in order to marry his second, pregnant bride Anne Boleyn are still being felt today.

The stock of rebel songs were predominantly written in the eighteenth and nineteenth centuries and consequently have English words. Patriotic songs sung in Irish are generally perversions of love songs.

A deep and abiding loathing of the English and the repression brought about by them is starkly apparent. *The Wearing of the Green*, which was written by Dion Boucicault (c. 1820–1890) rouses the fighting spirit alongside a bold spirit.

Then since the color we must wear is England's cruel
red,
Sure Ireland's sons will ne'er forget the blood that they
have shed;
You may take the shamrock from your hat, and cast it
on the sod,
But 'twill take root and flourish there, tho' underfoot
'tis trod.

Galway Bay remains one of the most poignant of ballads about the beauty of Ireland, written with real affection. Yet the telltale fourth verse of *Galway Bay* reveals the rebel nature of the writer.

For the strangers came and tried to teach us their way,
They scorn'd us just for being what we are,

But they might as well go chasing after moonbeams
Or light a penny candle from a star.

The systematic suppression of the Irish cost dearly in terms of human lives. There are a clutch of martyrs celebrated in song, including Rody McCorley.

The last verse reads:

Because he loved the motherland,
Because he loved the green
He goes to meet the martyr's fate
With proud and joyous mein;
True to the last, oh! true to the last
He treads the upward way;
Young Rody McCorley goes to die
On the bridge at Toome today

Poet Thomas Moore used the potent myths of old Ireland to embrace the nationalist spirit. Here are the words to *Let Erin Remember the Days of Old*:

Below: *Christy Moore has achieved fame world-wide with his predominantly traditional repetoire.*

Above: *Shane MacGowan, as lead singer with the London-Irish group The Pogues, made over some traditional classics for the modern market. Their hits include* A Pair of Brown Eyes, Sally MacLennane *and* Dirty Old Town.

Right: *Bono, of U2, in action on the Zooropa tour.*

Far right: *Dolores O'Riordan of The Cranberries in 1995.*

Danny Boy

Ask anyone outside Ireland about the song most evocative of the Gaelic melancholy spirit and the reply is invariably *Danny Boy*. Listening to the tragic story of the frail beauty whose sweetheart is called away to war when her own death is imminent sung to a melody heavy with grief and it is difficult to stay dry-eyed.

Yet those words were written by an Englishman, who probably never set foot on Irish soil. Look closely at the lyrics and there is nothing to root it in Ireland and few people born and bred in Ireland are acquainted with *Danny Boy*. They view it as a cultural cliché.

The lyrics were penned in 1910 by Frederic Weatherly (1848–1929), an Oxford scholar and English lawyer who used to write songs as a sideline, generally to fit existing music. Other Weatherly works include the words of *The Holy City* and *Roses of Picardy*. His melody failed to capture the imagination of audiences and the song faded and died.

It was revived two years later by Weatherly however, when he received from his sister-in-law in America a tune called *Londonderry Air* which fitted the *Danny Boy* words perfectly. So successful was the match between words and music that it became a major hit, particularly after being exported back to America where it was recorded by stars like Bing Crosby.

If the words were not Irish it seems the tune may have been, given its title. Yet even the name "Londonderry" implies some colonialist link as it was the name given by English and Scottish settlers to the region in the north of Ireland, an area the native Irish know as Derry.

Londonderry Air was among the tunes collected by George Petrie (1789–1866) for his publication *Ancient Music of Ireland*, which appeared in 1855. His source was a woman in Londonderry who contributed it without a

Below: *The splendor of the Irish landscape has inspired numerous writers to pen lyrics and melodies reflecting its glory. Pictured is the Twelve Bens in Co. Galway.*

title, claiming she notated it from the music played by a wandering piper. Thereafter it took the name of her home town.

However, the same tune was known by one or possibly two different names among the Irish community based in Chicago and appeared in the collection of music made there by Francis O'Neill at the close of the nineteenth century. Perhaps their inspiration was the undeniably Irish *Aislean an Oigfear* or *The Young Man's Dream* which bore an uncanny resemblance to *Londonderry Air* but dated back at least as far as 1840 when it appeared in *A Collection of Ancient Music of Ireland* gathered by Edward Bunting (1773–1843).

Students of the mystery are bound to admit that even the music of *Danny Boy* may emanate from outside Ireland. If the tune was common currency in Londonderry then it is as likely that it came from Scotland or England as Ireland, coming over with the planters who crossed the water in Elizabethan times.

Local legend has it that a man in Derry first found the tune. He fell asleep under a tree— and awoke to find a leprechaun sitting there with a violin playing the notes which are now so familiar as *Danny Boy*.

Above: *Another breathtaking scene, this time from Maam in Co. Galway.*

Whatever its origins, the notion that *Danny Boy* is a pure Irish thoroughbred is a hard myth to nail.

The Star of the County Down is another well-worn Irish favorite, made famous originally by John McCormack (1884–1945). Dublin-born McCormack achieved fame mostly in America and he became an American citizen in 1917. For his tireless charity work he was made a Papal count.

Finbarr Wright, an Irish tenor, discusses the present day popularity of the number. "It is a song which you hear very regularly performed by pop groups and rock groups. McCormack would never have expected that for a song that he discovered that is quintessentially an Irish ballad.

"It is always a lively tune so its always welcome. There seems to be a lot of slow ballads and slow songs generally so it's great to get one like that that gets the feet tapping. It is light, it is a little bit romantic and it's a very clever tune. Some lovely piano arrangements have been done to it over the years."

Let Erin remember the days of old
Ere her faithless sons betray'd her
When Malachi wore the collar of gold
Which he won from her proud invader
When her kings with standard of green unfurl'd
Led the Red-Branch Knights to danger
Ere the emerald gem of the western world
Was set in the crown of a stranger
On Lough Neagh's bank as the fisherman strays
When the clear cold eve's declining
He sees the round towers of other days
In the wave beneath him shining
Thus shall memory often in dreams sublime
Catch a glimpse of the days that are over
Thus sighing look through the waves of time
For the long-faded glories they cover

(Malachi was the king of Ireland in the tenth century who defeated two invading Danes in hand-to-hand combat, taking a collar of gold from one as a prize and a sword from the other.)

Far left: *Delores O'Riordan of the Cranberries sings* Zombie *during a show in Paris in November 1985.*

Above: *Members of Blackthorn reveal their mastery of traditional music on stage.*

Left and Overleaf: *The band Blackthorn, live on stage.*

Dancing

Above: *May day has always heralded celebrations, particularly dancing. This scene is dated May 1, 1780.*

Right: *Competitive dancing has been a prominent aspect of Irish culture since the start of the twentieth century. Immigrants took the pastime to America and it is there that this picture was taken.*

Think of Irish dancing and the music and movements of *Riverdance*, that phenomenally successful stage show, spring to mind.

Riverdance dancing is a remarkable reflection of Irish traditional dance. The dancers' head, body and arms remain almost motionless, leaving their legs and feet to tell a story in sequences of astounding speed and rhythm. The exhilarating sound is created by "treble" shoes, named after the noise they make.

Above: *A dance master with partner during New Year festivities in Ireland.*

Right: *An Irish jig danced to mark New Year's Day in 1870, to the strains of a piper.*

Above: *Two fiddle players provide the music for a summer's barn dance.*

It started life as a seven-minute stage routine to provide entertainment during the interval in the 1994 Eurovision Song Contest held at "The Point" in Dublin. Within months it had developed into a showbiz sensation. The rest is recent history.

But Irish dancing has a history far longer and more crucial than that of a single show.

As Michael Rooney from Comhaltas Ceoltóirí Éireann points out, "Irish music and dancing are intertwined.

"This was oral music passed down from generation to generation but its importance was as a social event. All the old music revolved around men, women and children playing for the neighbors or in their houses, or in the streets. Dancing was very much a communal social activity. It was all about people meeting up and having fun.

"Irish music is dance music," he continued. "Music was composed for the dances and vice versa. Even when there were no instruments people whistled. There are two or three different types of rhythm, all very fast and very lively. You feel compelled to tap your feet to the music. But the purpose of the music was to accompany dancing."

Like music, the early years of Irish dance have been lost. It is a familiar story—nothing was written down for posterity and the time-honored method of passing down dances by word of mouth came under stress during occupation.

It is known, however, that during Tudor times two Irish dances were popular enough to be exported to England. The Hey was a circular country dance or "round" and seems likely to have spawned a certain vein of English country dancing. The Trenchmore is the Anglicized name for the Rinnce Mor or Rinnce Fada, a long dance. In addition there were sword dances.

There is probably a shared ancestry between Irish, Scots, English and French dancing. Looking back from here it is difficult to distinguish who was first or best but it is likely that Irish dances were outstanding by their rapid tempo and the use of side steps.

The repression of the 1600s took its toll. Yet one contemporary observer claimed that country dancing remained commonplace on Sundays where there was, "in every field a fiddle and the lasses footing it till they are all of a foam." It is likely that the phrase "till the cows come home" came into usage to describe the enthusiasm and duration with which young people danced.

Remember that dancers risked not only the wrath of the occupying English but that of the Churchmen too, a mighty influence on their lives, who condemned dancing for the frenzy that it engendered.

In about 1750 a tradition began which assured the future of Irish dancing. Dance masters began travelling around the rural villages stopping off for a few weeks here, a month or two there, in order to teach the young people folk dancing steps.

They stayed with an amenable family—to be picked as host was a great honor—and taught on table tops in kitchens, in farm buildings, at crossroads or in hedge schools, the "underground," out-of-doors education system run by the oppressed Irish. Indeed, so often were dances held in the open air that one poem of the era dubbed Irish dancing as "tripping the sod." A dance master was often skilled in another lawful trade which provided his cover story should he be questioned by the authorities.

By the end of the third week it became usual to pay the Dance Master with the takings of what we now know as a "benefit" night. Musicians clearly had less stature. They were paid a week later.

Now the variety of dance steps multiplied. Each master taught recognized steps but added his own personal touches. He also might create new steps to old tunes. Competition among the dance masters was fierce. At countryside galas

Below: *Irish folk dancers giving a display at the English Folk Dance and Song Society in London's Regents Park in 1950.*

Right: *More Irish dancers in traditional dress, this time performing at the Festival of British Folk Dancing at Parliament Hill Fields in London. The year is 1953.*

Group Dancing

Set Dancing

Set dancing is the older of two types of group dancing. It descends from the courtly dances of Europe and has a dash of American square dancing thrown in for good measure. A full set comprises eight people, usually four couples, forming a diamond shape. It was, by tradition, danced at crossroads by the common people at the turn of the century. Rival cultural activities were created but set dancing remained popular, notably in County Clare. Recently it has enjoyed a revival.

Céilí Dancing

Céilí dances are junior to set dances. Dance masters contrived the Céilí movements at the behest of the Gaelic League which was concerned that existing step dances favoured by the people of Ireland were not "Irish" enough. Akin to the Scottish dances of the same name they were deemed far more middle class and respectable than set dances. These days Céilí dances and step dances are often mixed as part of an evening's entertainment.

Solo Dancing

Seán-nos dancing

Dances in Ireland once developed in isolation so regional styles and variations were strong. These have been greatly diluted although it is still possible to identify some. Old-style dancing is distinctive for its relaxed body stance. Arms may be loosely hanging by the sides, raised to waist level or even held above head height.

Step Dancing

Out of seán-nos dancing grew contemporary step dancing. It is the type of dancing which is judged at competitions held up and down Ireland and consequently the "rules" appear rather strict. Contemporary step dancers do not use their hands. The dancer's stance is upright and proud. The highlight is the footwork, generally more complex and skilled than sean-nos dancing. Costumes are equally important and the style is prescribed.

---

one might take on a rival to show just who knew the most dance steps. The audiences were rapt as dance masters, frequently clad in hats, swallow-tail coats, breeches and buckled shoes, danced themselves into a blur. It was quantity not quality that counted. Even the most expert dancer could lose out to the fellow with additional and original routines up his sleeve. The loser could find his "circuit" of villages given over to the triumphant winner, his personal standing and his income in tatters.

Eventually schools of dancing were created, the most dominant being in Cork, Kerry and Limerick. The style of dancing is now called sean-nos, which translates from Gaelic to mean old fashioned.

During the 1800s the craze was cake dances. Here a cake posted on a stand in the middle of the dance floor or field was the prize at a high spirited hooley. It went, of course, to the best dancer. An advertisement for just such a dance appeared in the *Dublin Evening Post* on October 1, 1734.

"On Thursday next, Mary Kelly, at the Queen's Head in Glasnevin, near this city, will have a fine plum cake, to be danced for by the young men and maidens of the country, who are generously invited by her, not doubting but they will be pleased with her ale as well as cake."

As Rooney points out, the dancing style of the time was not that mimicked by *Riverdance*.

"People using their whole body when they were dancing with arms swaying or even waved above their heads."

"After that there were dancing committees set up in the early 1900s. This is where step dancing came in. It was a totally different type of dance, entirely focussed on the legs. It was a very big discipline in which even having hands on hips would be out of the question."

This relatively recent change with the insistence of rigidity in the hands and arms may well have been a concession to the church whose-priests had long been unhappy at the sight of free movement during dance. So it seems the parish priests, unable to dent the popularity of dancing, insisted that arms were kept down by the dancers' sides. Dances were less abandoned this way and the dancers were showing some self control. It also happened that dances held indoors in front parlors and the like were so overcrowded that it made good sense to quell arm movements.

Irish-born Francis O'Neill wrote in his *Irish Folk Music* of 1910 that: "Traditional Irish music could have survived even the disasters of the Famine had not the means for its preservation and perpetuation—the crossroads and farmhouse dances—been capriciously and arbitrarily suppressed.

"'Twas done in my native parish of Caherea, West Carberry, in my boyhood days by a gloomy parish pastor. And the same senseless hostility to Irish music and pastimes was drastically enforced with a whip wielded by a P(arish) P(riest) on the backs of my nephews and their fellow revivalists."

Other changes were made in the dance traditions after the 1900s. This was the era of the Gaelic League, formed to bring all Irish national culture out of the closet. While once set dancing may have gone on among the native Irish behind

Below: *The discipline of young Irish dancers has often impressed audiences.*

Dance Music

There were jigs, which are thought to be the oldest surviving form of dance music. Musically speaking they are found in three forms, the single, the double and the slip jig. The double jig is the most frequently found of the three, with its 6/8 time. The single jig or slide is closely associated with the Sliabbh Luachra area of Cork of Kerry. It has a time signature of 12/8 and is much faster than the double jig. The slip jig, or hop jig as it is sometimes known, has a signature time of 9/8.

Popular jigs found today are the work of the fiddlers and pipers of the 18th and 19th centuries—although these may in turn have been based on previously known tunes. Carolan is the author of some of the best known.

The reel is more recent, arriving in Ireland from Scotland and played in 2/2 time. Most played today are of the mid-eighteenth century vintage. It is the most popular dance tune in the Irish tradition. And from England came the hornpipe.

closed doors now céilí held indoors at hotels and schools or outdoors at fairgrounds.

Formerly, solo dancing was at least as popular among men as women, if not male-dominated. Men would show bravado by dancing on soaped tables or rolling barrels and the jumps they used in dances were notably athletic. Teaching was entirely the preserve of men.

After the 1920s the balanced changed. Female solo dances, which had once been unknown, rose in number. Women became teachers and soon outnumbered the men.

Soft shoes came into use in the 1920s, too, where previously dancers had been barefoot. These would ultimately be replaced by hard shoes which these days have fibre glass toe tips and hollow heels. They may even be microphoned for special audio effect!

To celebrate their Irishness, pipers providing the dance music, and male dancers, wore kilts in the colors of Ireland; green, white and gold. Women favoured a white dress, coloured sash and hooded cloak or shawl on top. A tasseled cord dropped from the waist to the knees by way of decoration.

In 1936 the Irish government, with the backing of the Catholic Church, officially blacklisted home gatherings with the Dance Hall Act. This pushed dances into parish halls and paved the way for the first professional and semi-professional musicians.

It was primarily through dance that a significant new development in Irish music occurred, that of the céilí band. The inception of the céilí dates back to the turn of the century and the work of the Gaelic League. The first band to play for such dances is believed to have been formed in 1926 in the small parish of Ballina Kill in Galway. Without doubt the appeal of these bands was vastly increased by the power of radio from the Twenties onwards. It was influenced too by the enormous popularity of Irish-American dance halls in the States.

Céilí bands first played at public dances. Without modern amplification methods available to them the bands were of necessity loud and rhythmic. Traditional music for dances seemed to gain a few extra layers with its showband treatment—but no one minded when they were having so much fun. Only later when traditional music struggled to survive the onslaught of the céilí bands did resentment begin to grow.

Some of the famous names of the era were the Kilfenora Céilí Band, the Kincora and Castle Céilí bands. The Tulla Céilí Band has celebrated its fiftieth anniversary and it is estimated to have performed 3,000 live shows and seen 50 different players take up instruments in its name.

The céilí band lineup generally included several fiddle players, a couple of flautists, a piano, a button accordion and some drums. Irish music exported back to the mother country from musicians in America on radio or by gramophone records also featured the piano.

The bands— which each had a devoted following—became highly competitive.

Right: *Irish dancing taking place as part of the musical celebrations at Bru Boru in Cashel, Co. Tipperary.*

Ireland has also found itself deprived of all its first rate dancers, leaving the national competitions bereft of talent. All the best Irish dancers are in *Lord of the Dance* or *Riverdance* shows—out of the country on international tours.

Nevertheless, there is a generation of people who were compelled to learn Irish step dancing by their parents, to the hoots of derision of their classmates, who now find themselves vindicated.

Executive producer of *Riverdance*, Julian Erskine, admits that Irish dance was once burdened with a "nerd" image. The show, he says, has changed all that.

"It has allowed Irish dancers to hold their heads up with pride when before they might have been hiding their dance shoes in a plastic bag.

"It was and still is a competitive hobby. *Riverdance* employs over 100 Irish dancers full time, they are well paid, travelling the world, earning a living doing what is essentially their hobby. No longer are they the butt of jokes. Their friends are now envious, with people like Madonna and Jack Nicholson coming to see them perform.

"We in Ireland are known for our literary skills, we are known for our musical skills through people like U2, we were known briefly for our football skills and now there is Irish dance. The fact that *Riverdance* is doing so well is good for all Irish culture.'

The dancers bear out his theories. When Joanne Doyle was a teenager, she never admitted her passion for Irish dancing. Now she is revelling in the international acclaim it has won through *Riverdance*. "It was just a nerdy thing to do but everyone who kept it up did so because they loved it," says Joanne, who danced in three runs of the show in London. "*Riverdance* is a lovely pay off."

Joanne, from Dublin, was studying for her masters degree when she happened to tune in to that first Eurovision show. Having enjoyed Irish dancing since she was four, she was thrilled at the enthusiastic response and found herself hooked on the distinctive new dance. As soon as she finished her studies she joined a troupe preparing for the very first *Riverdance—The Show*. When the show is underway, the dancers meet twice a week to perfect their steps. They arrive at the theatre an hour and a half before curtain-up to go through muscle-toning exercises. At the end they mostly just want to stretch out and relax because, as Joanna puts it, "you are wrecked."

The intensity of the dancing has led to many injuries. During the final performance of the last London run, Joanne was sitting beside the stage watching one of the dances. When she got up, she felt a searing pain and found she had torn a cartilage in her knee.

"It had been a very long run—seventeen weeks—and you have to be so careful," she said. "I had an operation and didn't dance for ten weeks. I went with the company to New York, although I could only dance in one of the numbers. But my knee is grand now, touch wood."

Joanne understudies the lead parts, often pairing up with Breandan de Gallai for some of the Saturday matinées. Breandan, 26, was a relative latecomer to Irish dancing, starting at nine. Like many young dancers he was teased at school, although he didn't let his tormentors upset him. "They were people I didn't like, so I didn't care," he said. "And if it hadn't been the dancing it would have been something else as I was rubbish at football but played the flute, violin and piano."

After finishing secondary school, Breandan, from Donegal, won a scholarship to train for a year at a Chicago dance school, studying ballet, modern, jazz and tap. On his return, he spent four years studying applied physics at Dublin City University before going on to teach physics and maths at a Gaelic school for two years.

He took part in the Eurovision performance and jumped at the chance of joining the show. But he admits "I did get very sick in the middle of the first run, keeping up my day job, my night job—and the great social life that came with it all."

The show's emphasis has changed since the original lead dancer Michael Flatley left. "It made a difference but things would have changed anyway." Breandan says. "Colin Dunne, who took over, is a completely different dancer and he really added to the show."

Breandan is confident that *Riverdance* has a lasting appeal. "I think it is the freshness within all the dancers," he said. "Even numbers you have done 250 times still give you a tingle."

Irish step dancing is taught all over the world so the cast is not only confined to homegrown hopefuls. Colin Dunne, understudy to Michael Flatley, grew up in Birmingham, England, of Irish stock. He began Irish dancing at the age of four. By the age of nine he was the first person to win the All-Ireland, All-England and World Irish Dancing Championships in the same year. One of the *Riverdance* cast was born and trained in Australia. *Riverdance* fiddle-player Eileen Ivers was born in New York of Irish parents. A failed Irish dancer, she had violin lessons from the age of eight instead and went on to win the All-Ireland Fiddle Championships seven times.

Michael Flatley left *Riverdance* to launch his own show, *Lord of the Dance*. Irish traditional music is surely in the debt of both.

"The shows are popularising Irish cultural tradition. They are bringing people in all over the world who might otherwise never have encountered it," explains Niall Keegan.

Sales of Irish traditional music are reliably rock steady. While songs and groups may not be charging up the charts neither are they falling into oblivion, which is the fate of so many popular music artists.

It all rather gives lie to the advice given freely by Sir Arnold Bax: "One should try everything once, except incest and folk-dancing."

Below: *Music was fundamental to the success of* Riverdance. *Its band, Altan, won world-wide recognition.*

Timeline

400 B.C. Invasion by Celts. Ireland was divided into the five tribal kingdoms of Ulster, Meath, Leinster, Munster, and Connaught.

c. 390 A.D. Birth of St. Patrick (Feast Day: March 17. Emblems: Snakes and shamrock.)

c. 460 Death of St. Patrick, conversion of Ireland to Christianity.

1014 Battle of Clontarf. Brian Boru dies but Viking incursions are stopped.

1169 Arrival of the Normans. Within two years most Irish bishops and kings had submitted to their rule.

1366 Statute of Kilkenny, outlawing native Irish customs.

1641 Irish rebellion against Plantations.

1649 Oliver Cromwell arrives to suppress rebellion.

1726 *Irish Airs* published by John and William Neale in Dublin.

1738 Death of Carolan.

1742 Handel's *Messiah* premieres at Mr Neal's New Musick Hall in Fishamble street, Dublin.

Above: *At the fair in Kilarney, Co. Kerry.*

Right: *An awesome sight: Doonbriste, Downpartrick Head in Co. Mayo.*

1747 *Carolan's Collection* published in Dublin.

1762 Death of Italian composer Geminiani in Dublin.

1782 *Poor Soldier*, a ballad opera by William Shield, opens in Dublin.

1782 John Field, internationally known pianist, born in Dublin.

1792 Belfast Harp Festival.

1796 Bunting's *Ancient Irish Music* published.

1800 Act of Union. England strengthens hold in Ireland.

1807 Death of harpist Dennis Hempson.

1807–34 Moore's *Irish Melodies* is published.

1809 Bunting's *Second Collection* in print.

1828 *Beggar's Wedding*, the first Irish ballad opera by Charles Coffey is performed.

1829 Catholic emancipation.

1840 Bunting's *Third Collection* published.

1845 Irish Potato Famine begins.

1855 Petrie's *Ancient Music of Ireland* published.

1858 The Fenians, or Irish Republican Brotherhood, formed by James Stephens (1825–1901.)

1873 *Ancient Music of Ireland* published by Patrick Joyce.

1877 Petrie's second collection of 147 airs is published posthumously.

Left: William and James, the sons of a traveling tinsmith pictured in 1953.

1882 Thirty-nine further airs from Petrie are published with his notes.

1883 The Gaelic League, promoters of Irish national pride, is founded.

1884 Tenor John McCormack is born in Athlone.

1888 Joyce's second volume is published.

1889 Opera singer Margaret Sheridan is born in Co. Mayo, described by Puccini as "the ideal Mimi and the only Butterfly."

1905 *Complete Petrie Collection* of 1,582 tunes published by Sir Charles Stanford.

1907 Peadar Kearney composes "The Soldier's Song."

1909 *Old Irish Folk Music* by Joyce appears.

1916 Easter Rising. Fourteen leaders of the rebellion against the English were later executed.

1921 Irish Free State created.

1922 Free State prime minister Michael Collins is assassinated.

1949 Republic of Ireland proclaimed.

1951 Comhaltas Ceoltóiri Éireann formed to promote Irish traditional music, song, dance and language.

1971 Cumann Cheol Tire Éireann (Folk Music Society of Ireland) created to encourage Irish traditional music.

1971 Death of Seán Ó'Riada.

1994 *Riverdance* is staged in the interval of the Eurovision song contest, "seven minutes that shook the world."

1996 *Riverdance* opens at Radio City Music Hall in New York on St. Patrick's Day.

Festivals

February
Eigse an Phoball (West Belfast)

March
Arklow Music Festival (Co. Wicklow)
Irish Week at Bridge House
    (Tullamore, Co. Offaly)
Magherafelt Festival of Culture and the Arts
    (Co. Derry)
Feile na N-og Children's Festival (West Belfast)
Guinness Roaring 1920s Festival
    (Killarney, Co. Kerry)
St. Patrick's Day Festival (Dublin)
St. Patrick's Day Carnival Parade (West Belfast)

April
Kenmare Easter Walking Festival (Co. Kerry)
Rathdrum Easter Walking Festival (Co. Wicklow)
Sambhlaiocht Chiarrai (Co. Kerry)
International Pan Celtic Festival (Tralee, Co. Kerry)
Wexford Viking Festival (Wexford)
Emigrants Return Weekend
    (Manorhamilton, Co. Leitrim)
Feile na Bealtaine (Dingle, Co. Kerry)

May
Courtown Failte Festival (Co. Wexford)
Bealtaine Arts Festival (Newbridge, Co. Kildare)
Fair of Ballycumber (Co. Offaly)
Feile na Bealtaine (Letterkenny, Co. Donegal)
Heineken Green Energy Dublin International
Music Festival
Josie McDermott Memorial Festival
    (Co. Roscommon)
Tullaghbegley Mountain Walk
    (Falcarragh, Co. Donegal)

Feile na nDeise (Dungarvan, Co. Waterford)
Magherafelt and District May Festival
    (Co. Derry)
Kilmore Quay Angling Festival (Co. Wexford)
Ballyclare May Fair (Co. Antrim)
A Sense of Cork (Cork City)
French Irish Music Weekend
    (Collooney, Co. Sligo)
Northern Lights Festal
    (Ballcastle, Co. Antrim)
Vale of Avoca Melody Fair (Co. Wicklow)
Dundalk International Maytime Festival
    (Co. Louth)
Sligo Arts Festival (Co. Sligo)
Kenmare Whit Walking Festival (Co. Kerry)
Leixlip Festival (Co. Kildare)
Murphy's Cat Laughs Comedy Festival
    (Kilkenny)
Carrick-on-Shannon Community (Co. Leitrim)
Arts Festival Guinness Buttevant Arts Festival
    (Co. Cork)
Humours of Bandon Traditional Festival
    (Co. Cork)
Iniscealtra Festival of Arts (Co. Clare)

June
Eigse Carlow Arts Festival (Carlow Town)
Clonakilty Agricultural Show (Co. Cork)
Spotlight On Skerries Arts Festival (Co. Dublin)
New Ross Traditional Fair Day (Co. Wexford)

Right: *An Irish piper playing at the fair in Ballycastle,
Co. Antrim, in 1955.*

Ennis Arts Festival (Co. Clare)
Dunlavin Festival of Arts (Co. Wicklow)
Ferns Heritage Festival (Co. Waterford)
Kildare Derby Festival (Kildare)
Gem of the Roe (Dungiven, Co. Derry)
Durrus Community Festival (Co. Cork)
Mid Ulster Folk Festival
    (Moneymore, Co. Derry)
Annual Wolseley Festival (Tullow, Co. Carlow)
West Cork Chamber Music Festival (Co. Cork)

July

Liberties Festival (Dublin)
Coalisland International Music Festival
    (Co. Tyrone)
Willie Clancy Summer School
    (Milton Malbay, Co. Clare)
Donabate/Portrane Summer Festival
    (Co.Dublin)
Kells Heritage Festival (Co. Meath)
Duncannon Cockle Festival (Co. Wexford)
Salthill Harp Festival (Co. Galway)
Ballymahon Festival (Co. Longford)
Cashel Cultural Festival (Co. Tipperary)
Ballinode Heritage Festival (Co. Monaghan)
Tobber Curry (Co. Sligo)
Feile Arainn Mhor (Co. Donegal)
Achill Island Seafood Festival (Co. Mayo)
Ballina Street Festival (Co. Mayo)
Drumshaibo (Co. Leitrim)
Eileen Aroon Festival (Bunclody, Co. Wexford)
Mullingar Festival (Co. Westmeath)
Galway Arts Festival (Galway city)
Seachtain Charn Tochair (Maghera, Co. Derry)
Mullingar Bastille Day (Co. Westmeath)
Bandon Family Festival (Co. Cork)
Carndonagh Summer Festival (Co. Donegal)
Boyle Gala Festival (Co. Roscommon)
Kanturk Wild Boar Festival (Co. Cork)
Fiddle playing at Glen Colmcille (Co. Donegal)
Mountcollins Feile Cheoil (Co. Limerick)
Burtonport Summer Festival (Co. Donegal)
Lady of the Lake Festival
    (Irvinestown, Co. Fermanagh)

Left: *Irish musicians (l to r) Con O' Drisceoil, Johnny McCarthy, Paul O'Shaughnessy and Pat Ahern, in full flight.*

Buncrana Music Festival (Co. Donegal)
Iorras '98 (Ballina, Co. Mayo)
Ahiohill Community Festival (Co. Cork)
Durrow Carnival Weekend (Co. Laois)
Kilmacrennan Festival (Co. Donegal)
Brideswell International Celtic Festival
    (Co. Roscommon)
Des Carty Traditional Summer School
    (Tallaght, Co. Dublin)
Skibbereen Welcome Home Festival (Co. Cork)
Belturbet Festival of the Erne (Co. Cavan)
Easkey Summer Festival (Co. Sligo)
Mary From Dungloe International Festival
    (Co. Donegal)
International Darlin' Girl From Clare Festival
    (Co. Clare)
Mohill Arts and Summertime Festival
    (Co. Leitrim)
Wicklow Regatta Festival (Wicklow town)
Garnish Family Festival (Beara, Cork)
Grainne Ualle Festival (Newport, Co. Mayo)
Mitchelstown Music Festival (Co. Cork)
Wild Rose Festival
    (Manorhamilton, Co. Leitrim)
Ballyshannon Folk & Traditional Music Festival
    (Co. Donegal)

Waterford Spraio (Waterford city)
Greystones Summer Festival (Co. Wicklow)
Loughglynn Woodlands Harvest Festival
    (Co. Roscommon)
Muff Festival (Co. Donegal)
O'Carolan Harp & Traditional Music Festival
    (Co. Roscommon)
Siamsa Sraide (Swinford, Co. Mayo)
Youghal International Busking Festival
    (Co. Cork)
Percy French Festival (Co. Cavan)
Dunmore (Co. Galway)
Gorey Summer Fair (Co. Wexford)
Arne Valley Festival (Co. Waterford)

August
International Maiden of the Mournes Festival
    (Co. Down)
Sneem Welcome Home Festival (Co. Kerry)
Clonmany Family Festival (Co. Donegal)
Feile an Phobail (West Belfast)
Lismore Community Festival (Co. Waterford)

Below: *Traditional musicians receive a warm welcome both in and out of Ireland.*